THE REAL ME

Uncovering, Discovering & Recovering You

SARAH MILLS

First published by Ultimate World Publishing 2023
Copyright © 2023 Sarah Mills

ISBN

Paperback: 978-1-922828-44-6
Ebook: 978-1-922828-45-3

Sarah Mills has asserted her rights under the Copyright, Designs and Patents Act 1988 to be identified as the author of this work. The information in this book is based on the author's experiences and opinions. The publisher specifically disclaims responsibility for any adverse consequences which may result from use of the information contained herein. Permission to use information has been sought by the author. Any breaches will be rectified in further editions of the book.

All rights reserved. No part of this publication may be reproduced, stored in or introduced into a retrieval system, or transmitted in any form, or by any means (electronic, mechanical, photocopying, recording or otherwise) without the prior written permission of the author. Any person who does any unauthorised act in relation to this publication may be liable to criminal prosecution and civil claims for damages. Enquiries should be made through the publisher.

Cover design: Ultimate World Publishing
Layout and typesetting: Ultimate World Publishing
Editor: Victoria Pickens
Illustrated by Sophie Clarke
Cover image copyright license: Creative Travel Projects-Shutterstock.com

Ultimate World Publishing
Diamond Creek,
Victoria Australia 3089
www.writeabook.com.au

This book is dedicated to my beloved children

Robert, William, Sophie, and Anna

Forever and always

And to David, my rock

With Gratitude and Love

Illustrations by Sophie Clarke

I wrote this book for me.

After the disappointment of a failed marriage and with four children I devolved into a tragic zombie, doing what I had to do, day to day, but in complete disconnect. I lost my way, I lost trust in myself. My outer life improved; I appeared 'together' and remarried a wonderful man, but the trust I used to have in myself, to know myself and what was right for me, didn't return easily. How could I know anything if I couldn't 'save' my family?

I turned to philosophy, psychology, curiosity, my Yoga practice, and my interminable need to ask questions to explore getting back to The Real Me. As the book came together, I realised that others may benefit from my journey and was inspired to re-design it as a course.

Right now I'm a Realer, a more compassionate me than I have ever been. I can't tell you how to do this; I am not you, and your path, challenges, and superpowers are unique. What I can do is guide you, bit by bit, to explore, uncover, discover, and recover your Real Me.

Come with me on an incredible journey of your own.

Sarah Mills

Contents

Why The Real Me?	1
Chapter 1: The Real Me: Not Lost, Just Buried - and Why	17
Chapter 2: This Is Me! Feel the Flow	33
Chapter 3: The Real Me, Naked and Now	61
Chapter 4: Tools for Embodying The Real Me	77
Chapter 5: The Real Me: Holy and Wholy and Holey	95
Chapter 6: Creating The Real Me	109
Chapter 7: Tapping Into the Superpowers of *The Real Me*	123
Chapter 8: Entering the Dagobah Cave; Lighting the Dark Corners of The Real Me	153
Chapter 9: Being The Real Me, Each and Every Day	193
Chapter 10: Running Away With The Real Me or Me, Next...	211
Chapter 11: The Real Me, Meet The Real You	233
Epilogue	247
Afterword	249
About the Author	255

Why The Real Me?

"Know thyself."
(Temple of Apollo, Delphi)

I don't know you, but I'm excited that you've picked up my book. *The Real Me* book in your hands is the culmination of a life of trial and error; searching for a deeper understanding of *who* I am and *why* I am the way I am. This is not the biography of my personal search; rather a road-map to help you reconnect with your own Me and release elements of your life which aren't really you at all.

I am me

And who you see

Is nothing but

The REAL me.

Who amongst us can say this?

The Real Me

As an introspective person living in a Western culture, which encourages us to both 'love yourself' and 'be yourself' whilst concurrently bombarding us with a million 'you are not enough' self-help propaganda blogs and posts, I have wondered and have existed in this bemusing space for years. These are the sorts of questions that have interested, intrigued, and frustrated me over a lifetime:

- *"Just be yourself."* But what even *is* that?
- If I could strip away all the stuff I've been taught, coached and (sometimes) forced to be, how much of me would remain?
- Why am I drawn to certain things/activities/people and from where do my interests and natural abilities stem?
- Does *The Real Me* even exist - Is it important or even necessary to be *The Real Me*?
- How much of MeRightNow is The Real Me and how much is parental and societal teachings? (Ultimately designed to make me more manageable and fit in, yet perhaps not allow me to experience myself as *The Real Me* at all?)
- What am I here to do?
- Who am I underneath all my habits and thoughts?
- What one thing don't I know that will have the most effect on my life?

Yes, I'm always asking questions!

As a high school science teacher, I once asked colleagues: *"When does being a teacher go from what you do to what you* are? I **am** a teacher? *Rather than I teach, that's what I do?"*

They gave me a look as if to say: *"Hmmm; you're a strange one."*

Indeed.

Why The Real Me?

One of my goals for this book is encouragement; me encouraging you. I've discovered that a big part of *The Real Me* (Sarah, that is) is encouraging myself and others to examine new ideas, inquire into themselves, and explore life from different perspectives. Alongside this, I identify with being the cheer squad, listening ear and the soft place to fall, if and when others need it. I don't have all the answers, but I love connecting, probing, and exploring best practice with others – with you.

As both a teacher and student, much personal experience, self-illuminating practices, reading and Life has condensed me into *The Real Me* – both personally, and this book. I decided to write *The Real Me* in the first person whilst weaving in the occasional second and third person as I really want YOU to consider this road-map course of self-enquiry to be about yourself, personally. Firsthand.

Experience is understanding, and this understanding is about me, by me, my experiences, what I relate to, what I think I know, and what I feel.

So, this book is about *You*...as *Me*.

Understanding ourselves at a deeper level has been a human imperative for millennia. Yet we possibly know our best friend or close colleague better than we know ourselves. We can be terrified of delving deep into our own passions, priorities and neuroses. In our hectic, information-saturated age, this quest is more important than ever before. It takes work and commitment. Welcome to *The Real Me* journey.

> *"Yet, who is the real I, where does he hide from ME? I know who he is not, but how and what and if at all HE is, I have never discovered although for more than seventy years I have been looking for him."*
> *(Berenson)*

Igniting The Real Me

Being your authentic self is the best gift you can give both yourself and everybody else in your life.

Welcome. You've picked up this book because there are elements of your life in which you suspect: *"I'm not showing up as The Real Me."*

It comes as a hunch or a feeling – or maybe more of a slap in the face when you find yourself speaking or behaving as someone you don't - or worse, do - recognise – and you have a moment of deep questioning. Or, perhaps life is becoming overwhelming, and you feel as if you are lost in a life which has evolved and has a momentum, but somehow doesn't reflect you at all. You might have noticed whispers – or you might be into the full-on screams! You might be wearing so many different hats that it's become difficult for the real authentic person beneath them to make herself or himself known. How do you hear that small *real* voice above the clamour of all the information, tasks, jobs and demands that are placed on you, from day to day?

This book will take you on a path of excavating *The Real Me*; the important, purposeful elements of yourself that bring you satisfaction and contentment; moment to moment, day to day, leading into weeks, months and long term. So, along with the challenges and the points of interest you experience in each and every day, you can join me in saying: *"I really feel as if I'm Me in this lifetime amongst all the complexities, challenges and joys. Amongst all the incredible things that I still want to do and all the interesting things I've done, I feel that at the end of every day, that I've lived today as Me."*

In this course, you will explore many of the elements which make up *The Real Me*; some will be obvious to you and others a real blindside; these, of course, are the exciting (and sometimes scary) revelations!

Why The Real Me?

Don't be surprised when friends have a completely different experience than you with this course; we are all born with a unique set of skills to develop and have varying interests. We also have our own unique ways of making our full contribution to society in this lifetime. If you're still muddling about, as I've been for much of my life, trying to figure out what your purpose is and how to live your life the most authentic way — and really wanting to — then it's time to dive in

> *"That is the point of the night sea journey—to be born into yourself. There, you are in the amniotic fluid, in an alchemical substance once again. You are journeying toward your own life. You are preparing for your fate. The promise is exhilarating, but the dangers are extreme. You have to avoid being just one of the crowd, and instead take the chance of being born an individual."*
> *(Thomas Moore)*

At this point, please note that *The Real Me* is simple, but not easy. Your journey of yourself, by yourself, into yourself may not be the tiptoeing through the tulips exercise that we hope it might be. There will be some dark corners and potential 'bogs of eternal stench' that you uncover in your own Labyrinth, deep beneath your carefully constructed semi-façade of *Me*. You are the only person who can discover and recover your *Real Me*; the only person who can be your *Real Me* and thus live your life as the fullest, largest unfettered version of your *Real Me*. You are the only person who can do this work.

Your work to discover and live as *The Real Me* - your real *Me* - is vital not only for your personal highest wellbeing, but also in the particular way that you can enrich the lives of others and benefit our world. You are irreplaceable and your contribution to our planet and its inhabitants is one of a kind.

The Real Me

Understand that *The Real Me* has always been within you, waiting for you to undertake this journey into yourself. You *want* to be excavated, unburied, and unleashed. And you simply can't do it wrong.

The Real Me Inquiry Process; asking, listening and trust

This is a course of inquiry. After all, only you can know how great it feels when you actually live each day as *The Real Me*. So, there are no right answers, but there are many questions.

An inquiry course brings progress and change simply because you're not being told what's right or told what to do (a key indicator that you are carefully toeing someone else's *Me*). Sure, there are plenty of ideas presented in this book and some may resonate with you – these are the important ones – but inquiry is finding the answers for yourself within yourself.

Listening. Trusting. Opening.

Have you ever been advised that everything you are looking for is 'out there'? Not likely. The message from all sages from Jesus to the mystics is that when looking for ourselves and deep truths, turn within.

> *"The Universe is not outside of you. Look inside yourself; everything that you want you already are."*
> *(Rumi)*

> *"The kingdom of God lies within you."*
> *(Luke 17:20-21)*

Can we even consider that we already are The Real Me when we've been brought up with the secular notion of 'tabula rasa'; that we're

Why The Real Me?

born knowing nothing, a blank slate for everyone to write on? That we studiously must learn everything? Our learnings are of course, important and give us context, but for now, let's consider the idea that instead we are born with a deep inner knowing and connection to all things. It's just an idea, you don't have to believe it. Bring to mind activities you love and are naturally drawn to, even as a very young child? Nourishing friends you choose to connect with; books or posts you choose to read over others? Could these be part of your inner guidance? Let's explore.

"A prudent question is one half of wisdom."
(Francis Bacon)

Inquiry works by asking yourself a question – out loud or in your head, word for word, and then pausing. Notice what comes up from inside you. All the answers are there, and the answers may change if you ask at different times. Answers may change as you excavate more deeply. Answers may change as your understanding of the question (and your responses) change.

Trusting in The Real Me

Our inquiry starts with a powerful Question:

Q: *"Do I trust my own answers?"*

Ask yourself this question either out loud, in a murmur, or in your head. Word for word.

When you ask yourself this or any intuitive question, notice what happens in your mind.

Does time slow down? Is there a space created in which nothing happens and there's no response? You may suddenly notice your breath, then after a moment you wonder: *What was the question?*

Or is there an immediate answer? Is it the response you expected? Can you enquire more deeply?

Trust is to believe that someone is good and honest and will not harm you, or that something is safe and reliable (Cambridge) and is part of the 90% of our lives which is invisible (Caroline Myss). We have conscious and unconscious criteria we use to decide the trustworthiness of others, but trust of ourselves can be variable. Trusting ourselves is a *continuum* with a healthy balance somewhere towards the 'I'm Trustworthy' end. Consider that the lens we use to observe ourselves may be too close for good focus and we might not see the Wood for the Trees. We may have made mistakes and broken promises. This has taught us to doubt our personal trustworthiness. At the same time, these experiences may have strengthened our trustworthiness muscle so that we may be more dependable now than we've ever been, yet our lens is still clouded.

Conversely our self-trust may be ironclad; we may always do and behave in a responsible way and never doubt our inner voice and gut feelings. Even when shown to be wrong, we might learn *from* this but not learn self-doubt. If that's you, skip the next paragraph. If your response to the powerful trust Question brought a variable response and some emotion, consider having a full-on conversation with yourself about this one point:

Q: 'Do I trust myself?'

Inquiry never feels super-comfy, so always ask yourself if you can inquire further. Further inquiry allows supporting or more probing questions to arise. 'Do I trust myself?' can perhaps expand into:

Why The Real Me?

Can I trust myself? How and when? When did I last have my best interests at heart? How did I learn not to trust myself? Can I pinpoint when it started? How do things generally turn out when I do trust myself? When I allow others to decide for me?

This may trigger a pain point so that you can begin to observe and release part of your Not Me armour. Breathe. If you have extended this **Q**, you are already beginning to excavate the trust that is *The Real Me*, your birthright and your authentic self. It's a shining light that you, likely with the help of others, have dumped or concreted over. Listening to your inner voice and trusting is a healing process in itself. Maybe finish by asking yourself: 'Who do I want to be?' You are that person, right now. Rest, smile and breathe.

All Inquiry is Voluntary

Instruction Manual for The Real Me:
How to use this course:

Each chapter has at least one set of inquiry questions. Choose your approach.

Systematically, you may like to work through each question, one at a time. Allow each question a few moments and close your eyes if you like. Try saying the **Q** aloud and mentally. Which do you prefer? Some people like to repeat the question three times or more. Consider the response that you observe. Observing is a skill in itself, especially for those of us who have a Master's Degree in ignoring ourselves and sidelining our own needs. Be patient. Keep in mind that observing is much more than our five senses.

The Real Me

Your observed response may be:

1. Feeling or emotion. Pay attention to strong emotions. Some **Q** bring me straight to tears, others openness and joy.
2. Physical sensation: you might find yourself nodding or shaking your head without realising, smiling, pursing lips, forehead lifting or frowning, body shifting position, gut feeling, tension or relaxing of any part your body. Your body is a wonderful megaphone for what's happening within. More in Chapter 4.
3. Word/words: Yes, No, Sometimes, Occasional, Never! Or other words may bubble up. Notice your commitment to a Y/N response as a clue to whether it's The Real Me or long-term coaching of what you *should* say.
4. Number or percentage: you may be a numbers-person or sometimes it may be a 50/50 or 80% response.
5. Breath response: you may gasp, sigh, or your breathing may change.
6. Image or colour: colours or images may hold special messages for you.
7. A flashback of a scene from your past, familiar or unusual, or from a movie. If it's painful, allow space and a few moments to sit with what's come up. Allow compassion and no judgement.
8. A person or people come to mind. Explore.
9. Part of a descriptive story or narrative?
10. Or a No Response. A blank will usually indicate a block, don't worry; it's a point to keep coming back to with compassionate interest.
11. You may experience a subtle or different *response*.

As you work through the course, notice which response/s emerge consistently for you. Or you may notice a combination, for example

Why The Real Me?

image *and* emotion. Does it depend on the Question? Or how long you spend on an inquiry?

- If you choose, return to the earlier question **Q:** ***"Do I trust my own answers?"*** in light of the above possible responses. What type of response did you note? Did your response change or become more refined?

Listen with awareness. When you ask the question, you increase your receptivity to the answer. Be open.

You may find yourself extending the line of inquiry from any particular question in this course. Extension generally comes in the form of 'Why.' 'Why?!?' can sometimes feel blamey; if so, place a personal boundary not allowing blame or shame. Any Why extensions are best as "Hmm...I wonder Why". You may like to write or draw your response in any meaningful way. You may like to ponder for a moment and consider any deep or real truth in the response. Alternatively, you may be drawn to a particular question *or* find yourself deliberately skipping a question(s). You can inquire as to why, or just go with it. You're the boss.

Allow the process to be fun and interesting, rather than scary and worrisome. After all, you're getting to know your best friend!

It is what is, you are what you are, both right now, as well as what you really are beneath your concrete, armour, and glamour/war paint.

Whether we choose to see it or not, as we refine our perceptions, awareness and understanding of ourselves through the course, we change, deepen and refine. *As we learn to be okay with The Real Me, we emerge.*

The Real Me

"We cannot change what we are not aware of, and once we are aware, we cannot help but change."
(Sheryl Sandberg)

It's time to play! Let's start with these broad Key Inquiry Questions. We will return to these in eleven weeks for you to celebrate how much Me you've unleashed! Remember, take one **Q** at a time. Take your time.

Key Inquiry Questions

Q: Do I love my life? In this moment? In general?
Q: Do I love myself?
Q: Am I willing to explore the idea of *"I'm simply not where I need to be right now and maybe I don't even know where that is?"*
Q: Am I willing to explore giving myself permission to be myself? Am I fearful of what I might expose?
Q: Can I even consider living life as my most authentic self; If no, are there some clues as to why not?
Q: Do I deserve a full, satisfying, and authentic life?
Q: Can I use every day as part of the exploration of building success and staying with it?

Notice how these are all yes/no/maybe/sometimes questions. Note the resounding YES's. Generally, *"yes"* feels good when it emerges. The *"no's"* or the *"I'm-not-sures"* or the "20%s" carry a different quality to them - If any arose for you, did you notice? What other styles of response did you notice? We'll explore these feelings and responses more in Chapter 1.

Remember, this is your life and it's not selfish to make being You a priority. You are here on this Earth for one reason only: to find your purpose and live your purpose. Our incredible existence demands

Why The Real Me?

more than eating, procreating, and somnambulating our way through life. I'm talking about the exciting, but not overwhelming, portfolio of reasons you get out of bed in the morning. Living *your* future and learning to trust *your* Real Me starts right now. Discovering creative passions you've put a lid on, features of your life you're totally scared to face, and parts you've buried mostly through coaching and fear. Talents and interests you "never get around to" enjoying or developing, elements of your life in which you don't seem to be succeeding, blind spots where you just don't know what you don't know.

This is what *The Real Me* is all about. Together, we're taking a really deep, long, loving, probing, opening interest in yourself; *The Real Me*, for the benefit of living your most fulfilling life as well as for your family, children, friends, community and the planet.

Consider making a commitment to work through the process: making the commitment Right Now because ultimately, it's a commitment to yourself. This doesn't mean you have to work with everything in this book. There may parts of it that you may skip over or choose only to work with two or three items or questions at a time. Piecemeal is fine, this is *your work at your pace*.

Or you may choose to work through the whole process; page by page, day by day, week by week for the whole eleven weeks. You may work in fits and starts over months. You may well return to certain parts (or come back to parts that you skipped – or within which you felt blocked at a previous time) as you're working through the course. **Just keep coming back**; keep coming back to the process and you'll watch yourself unfold and blossom.

> *"Change Your Questions, Change Your Life."*
> *(Marilee Adams)*

Being your authentic self is the best gift you can give both yourself, and everybody else in your life. Let's do it!

THE COMMITMENT:

I am *The Real* _____ *(enter your name)*, perhaps scattered or buried or ignored. I am ready to do the work; the consistent work of asking questions, trusting, and paying attention; allowing *The Real Me* to emerge piece by piece into the light; into my Real life.

Signed: _____ date: _____

Why The Real Me?

Who else can I be but **The Real Me?**

Only I can see who I might be.

Who made me? So many, I see.

Who can find me?

Only I can find **Me.**

So, I'll look inside and perceive

The Still Small Voice which is me;

The Powerful creative Voice which is Me

And live simply, beautifully

Graciously,

And gratefully as **The Real Me.**

Chapter 1

The Real Me: Not Lost, Just Buried - and Why

> *"We do not see things as they are,
> we see things as we are."*
> *(Anais Nin)*

Why DO we live our lives the way we do and why DO we believe what we believe – especially the beliefs about ourselves? We are shaped by culture, experiences and *so* many other people. How much of me is Me? And does it even matter? Aren't we all a mish-mash of a zillion things?

First, consider that your mission in this lifetime is to express *The Real Me* in the fullest, most beautiful, authentic and creative way possible. Perhaps this is your only purpose, and only you can do

The Real Me

this work because your unique talents and experiences make for a unique *You*.

This is your Quest, should you choose to accept it: to energize, discover, uncover, and recover *The Real Me* and find the authentic contentment and joy which are your birthright.

Next, consider *letting go* of the belief that *The Real Me* is something you have to find, develop, or build; we're going to explore the insidious belief that there is stuff *out there,* material things or knowledge that you need to add to yourself to somehow make you better. The *"I'm not enough"* philosophy that is pervasive in many cultures and on which advertisers have capitalized for years.

You are already you and it's already all there.

Over your lifetime, *The Real Me* has been, blocked, shunned, ignored, and shamed. And whilst you've tried to construct the life you assumed you wanted - or were told/shown you should have - your *Real Me* has waned like a plant denied sunlight, or buried beneath an inflexible, shiny, but less real *Me*.

There are good reasons behind your concrete, armour, and dilution: quite simply, self-protection. There have been pain points in your life where you've suddenly realized that your underbelly was exposed. Or worse; cut, boxed, and handed back to you. You've been hurt, embarrassed, and let down by people you thought had your back. And then you've been hurt some more. You've cried and resolved to be stronger, not to let the Bastards get you down, never to feel like *that* again. Armour. When you made mistakes and needed help to understand your own wrongdoings you were smashed rather compassed. More Armour. You may have hurt others whilst in your own pain. More Concrete. You may have suffered abuse beyond what I can understand. Some people around you did their best and some really not. You've blamed them, you've blamed yourself. You've become used to the armour, concrete, smiling and hiding. This has been my life, as well as yours and everybody on the planet's experience.

Your burying of The Real Me has come in spades and bunkers from feeling unsafe, in situations you may not even consciously remember. Thus your excavation, laying aside bits and chunks of concrete and armour, must come from your feeling safe in your exploration and at your own pace. *You* choose the exercises and questions, with which to engage and *The Real Me* practices will allow you to reconnect with Yourself in a variety of situations whilst exploring a variety of ideas. All within the boundaries of safety. If you don't want to go there, don't. You can come back to any part or inquiry later. Remember, the process will feel uncomfortable at times but must feel safe. As you progress through difficult parts of the course, ask yourself,

Q: Do I feel Safe? Is this unsafe or merely difficult?

Always come back to safe. Over time, you'll discover that letting go of what's *not* Me is the only way to discover and reconnect with what *is* me. Simple – but not easy.

This is one of my all-time favourite quotes, and ultimately inspired this book:

> *"Healing may not be so much about getting better, as about letting go of everything that isn't you – all of the expectations, all of the beliefs – and becoming who you are."*
> *(Dr Rachel Naomi Remen)*

The Real Me

Your job right now is simply to ask, listen, learn to trust, and *pay attention*. Then to really listen some more. Then let your own Sunshine illuminate *You*. It takes practise, attention, more attention and more practise.

Unbury Yourself

Throughout the course, *allow the inquiry process to give you permission to excavate.* Inner heavy lifting can be as exhausting as physical excavation, so allow time to consider, process and rest.

Whilst you're excavating, notice, allow and accept The Real Me as it emerges.

How do we notice parts of ourselves firmly wedged in our blind spots? How do we accept elements of ourselves we've been stomping on for years? This will take some practise. We'll work through the process together and your task is to keep coming back to it. Acceptance takes practise, awareness, and more practice.

Acceptance is a skill and as I tell my students, *any skill can be learned...but you have to practise.*

Throughout the course we'll learn to bypass and release your mental models of what you *think* is you and connect with what really *nourishes* you. We'll lovingly explore expanding you, from the current emaciated version of yourself, into a robust and full-bodied you.

In this book, we'll be behaving similarly to Socrates and Plato who continuously questioned (and annoyed) citizens of Athens about why they lived their lives the way they did. Why did you say that?

The Real Me: Not Lost, Just Buried – and Why

Why are you rich or poor? How did you know this? Are you a decent person? Are humans inherently selfish? Most often, citizens who allowed themselves to be questioned came to a point where they contradicted themselves or just couldn't answer. If this happens to you, please chuckle; it's fine.

We begin the journey into and towards *The Real Me* by asking some simple questions and kick-start the process of self-observation. We're getting to know ourselves from the inside out. Useful questions invite both deep reflection and deep feelings, with scope for more questions arising. We're asking meaningful questions with many possible answers.

Whilst working through this and subsequent chapters, be sure to read, observe and act upon the exercises with which you feel compelled – or curious. The inquiry questions are marked with the letter "**Q**". You will also find some rhetorical but open questions on which you may choose to ponder.

You are invited to very simply ask yourself questions and allow answers to arise.

Answers will come in those moments after you have read a **Q** or perhaps during the day as you're doing your chosen activities, or during moments of quiet. Keep asking, and allow these questions to settle deep. Noticing answers that come up is the main part of the inquiry process, as is paying attention to the process itself.

Trust is our first skill, and we're practising it. Trust and believe that The Real Me really is in there somewhere and delighting in your engagement with this process.

The Real Me

Returning to Anais Nin, seeing things as *we* are presupposes *looking out*. *The Real Me* process is about *looking in*. No matter which way we're looking, we are filtering all our observations through a lens of our own perception. Perceptions are defined as *"the way in which something is regarded, understood, or interpreted."* (Oxford Dictionaries, 2020)

We know that children are excellent observers but poor interpreters – as big kids, could this also be true of *Us*? In some areas more than others? The *something* in Oxford's definition is, of course: *Me*. Our perceptions allow us to define ourselves as individuals. But what if many of our current perceptions of ourselves are outdated, misguided, serving others rather than our fullest selves, or simply plain wrong?

Together, we're going to inquire as to how we have created our perceptions about ourselves and examine our attachment to them. We'll interrogate, recognise, refine, accept, as well as discard many of them during this process. Whilst your *Real Me* may encapsulate some of your current perceptions and beliefs, many are not *The Real Me* at all. The accepted untruths of our lives and societies have limited and diminished us.

These perceptions can be strong and deeply rooted; many of these you'll have long accepted as truth – about yourself, others, and the world around you. If you feel, at least sometimes, lost, overwhelmed, and often left wondering why doing all the things that we're told to do to live a happy, successful life aren't leaving you feeling grounded, healthy, or happy, then you are not alone. Your foundation principles and perceptions may be more smoke and mirrors than supportive and nourishing. Or perhaps they are supportive to others, but not you.

The only true wisdom is in knowing you know nothing.
(Socrates)

The Real Me: Not Lost, Just Buried - and Why

Let's begin at ground zero by considering the idea that, *nothing you think you know is true.*

It's just an idea; an expansive idea. You don't have to believe it; just consider it. It's a scary proposition, but also incredibly liberating. This includes your thoughts and beliefs, those *belonging to* you and particularly, those you believe *about* yourself or about others. Are my thoughts and beliefs the same thing? When are/aren't they? Where do my beliefs come from? Nuclear family, education systems, religious teachings, culture, friends, books, podcasts? My own experiences? Our societies are becoming further polarized, and as people are more likely to be attracted to others who already have similar beliefs, how can we feed ourselves an omnivorous diet of ideas? Is truth even a thing?

Generally speaking, our minds simply struggle to compute a really expansive idea; such ideas blow our minds and eyes wide open (ever experienced a moment of 'no mind'?) The other option is that we simply dismiss it. How can we begin to comprehend the suffering and death of over six million Jews during WWII? We can't. Nothing is real until you've experienced it. Intellectualising and reading about ideas does not make them real to you. And we're all about Real.

Any expansive idea which resonates with you I'll call a Deep Truth. We might not fully grasp the depth or application, but it has a particular quality of feeling about it. It *feels* true. Deep truths have a way of echoing far within *The Real Me* in ways that bypass our bean-counter of a mind. You may or may not have recognised the idea of nothing you think of as being true as a Deep Truth. Throughout this course you will find a quote, idea or sentence that stops you in your tracks. Incredible beauty has the same effect. Have you ever encountered a scene so beautiful that for a moment, your mind, breath and even time stood still?

The Real Me

Take note of your Deep Truths as they arise. Your truths may be different from those of others. You may wish to keep a journal and note down ideas, Deep Truths, and your particular response to them. At this point, I'd like you as an explorer of both life and yourself to undertake a pledge:

Never take anything at face value. Question (not judge) everything. This includes your thoughts, actions, your beliefs, the way you live your life, how others live their lives. And by taking this approach, you'll start to notice everything. Not all at once, but you'll begin to start observing yourself and your life in a different manner, much like a primary school student with a new project. You have a Project.

And You're it.

This week we're starting slow. Our task is to simply observe your *Real Me,* just as you are now and question *what I do* and think, *and why;* in the way that an inquisitive child might buzz around you and ask:

"Why are you doing this? Why are you doing that?"

Yes, you're really out to annoy yourself with your own observation. To each question, really consider - is there an answer/answers? If so, what might it be now? Later it may be different.

Remember that within the general busy activities of life, society approved learned behaviours, habits, and overthinking, our *Real Me's* tend to be buried, clouded and scattered to the four winds. Recall that the process of uncovering *The Real Me* is an excavation process, designed to bring clarity and potency to your life. It also involves a willingness to dig into those dark corners of yourself which may well bring you discomfort. This is done with support through the process as well as you deciding the pace and what you are ready to tackle. You are firmly in the driver's seat.

Take a big, open exhale and smile. Are you ready? ☺

Assignment for Chapter 1

Every day this week, as you go about your daily routine – or perhaps, something out of your routine – take a few moments to question, then question some more.

Q: "Why am I doing this?"

You'll have hundreds of opportunities to ask yourself this question, just in one day, so hone in on a few only; maybe six to twelve times today, then a few more tomorrow, then a few more. **The practice is not to change anything that you choose to do**, but simply to notice WHAT you choose to do and interrogate WHY. Here is an example and some follow up questions:

Q: Why am I doing this?

For example, making your morning coffee or tea. Why? *Because I always make a coffee first thing.* Why? *To help me wake up, to get me going to make me feel alive.* Why? *Just because!*

Why? *I don't know, I just love it!*

Q: What would happen if I didn't? Did you notice that mental arrest or pause? Mental Space? That sense of "I don't know what would happen if I didn't." Then an answer may arise.

The Real Me

Q: Whatever I'm doing right now - is this habit or purposeful?
Going to the bathroom – definitely purposeful. Eating – am I hungry or habitually eating?
Am I busy working/scrolling on social media/watching TV/_____ to pass time until I can _____ or to avoid _____? (fill in the blanks here)

Here are some tougher Q. Choose 1 or more to engage with. Remember, all inquiry is voluntary.

Q: Which elements of my day-to day routine have real meaning at present? *Choose a couple or more.*
Q: Which elements of my life have real meaning at present? *A more holistic question.*
Q: If I could be doing anything in the world right now, what would it be? *Yes, anything. What & Why?*
Q: What really challenges me? Do I accept it or avoid it? *Small or large challenges, you choose.*
Q: What little things really bug, bother, needle or annoy me? *If I'm going to explode over something trivial, what is it?*

Some questions you may find yourself answering easily, others may bring up a feeling of defensiveness; others may hang with no answer arising. In a society where questions demand answers, this may feel uncomfortable. Notice if you can allow and accept some hanging questions. This is a great way to practice simple acceptance of the unknown and of mental space around an inquiry. Sometimes if you jump in too quick, it can be a sign of a coached response rather that *The Real Me*. Notice if you find yourself pursuing answers to some questions and reach a block or are simply distracted by the next thing to do.

Of course, any response - or no response at all - is part of the process of learning to pay attention to yourself. During the first few days, you'll likely find yourself forgetting to notice for hours at a time!

Hopping off The Judgment Juggernaut

Notice if you immediately jump to making judgments:

How well have I done at this inquiry task? (Who are you measuring yourself against? Are you keeping score of how many times you noticed and asked why? Are you using technology to assist – setting a timer to remind you?)

Did I deliberately choose to *not* notice certain activities? Interesting.

Did I forget to notice for hours at a time and started berating myself?

Did I decide the task is stupid anyway?

By all means, make assessments, with a detached sense of "that's interesting," but notice when assessing descends into darker, personal judgments: *"Why didn't I? I can never... Oh, I can't believe I did THAT again!"*

If you notice negative self-judgment, bring yourself back into the light. This week we're intensely interested in what we are doing, not doing, and why, but beating ourselves up can be a longstanding habit. Notice it, of course, but do NOT allow your self-observation to be hijacked by negativity. Be prepared even for these assessments to be let go as deeper understandings come.

The Real Me

Do you find yourself defending your own responses? To yourself? Lol, for example: *"I don't have to answer to YOU as to why I'm having that second glass of wine!"*, or perhaps, mentally complaining about a co-worker or family member; 'I *can* say/think that! They let me down.' Or what about not getting up early to exercise today; 'I just didn't have time, slept in, didn't feel like it' ... Interesting, isn't it? (These are some of mine, of course!)

Consider that rarely does one single question or assessment provide you with immediate clarity; a sense of *me* revealed, ready to live with joy and purpose! A single question or point of truth may be the opening of *Pandora's Box* and equally, it may be fine tuning or simply discarded as irrelevant. Notice with care and curiosity if all/most of your responses are somewhat vague, with no real surprise or follow-up questions. Elements of our current state of mind will be very keen to keep us in the status quo and may resist probing. Notice - and keep on probing.

> *"Life is a journey and it's about growing and changing and coming to terms with who and what you are and loving who and what you are."*
> *(Kelly McGillis)*

Why? Why? Why?

We choose a hundred different things a day and within our choices lie our ability to recover or uncover our authentic self.

> *"Our true selves are akin to continuously writing a poem."*
> *(Xunwu Chen)*

The Real Me: Not Lost, Just Buried – and Why

We can develop or intuit an intention to uncover, discover and recover our authentic self. Starting in this moment, as a line in the poem of our life, we will journey towards *The Real Me*.

As far as I know, there is no formal field of study of inquiry so let's examine the basic premise of inquiry and how it serves our unfurling of *The Real Me*. John Barrell's Developing More Curious Minds outlines the following criteria for inquiry:

- A good question is an invitation to think (not recall, summarize, or detail).
- A good question comes from genuine curiosity and confusion about the world.
- A good question makes you think about something in a way you never considered before.
- A good question invites both deep thinking and deep feelings.
- A good question leads to more good questions.
- A good question asks you to think critically, creatively, ethically, productively, and reflectively about essential ideas.
- Good questions encourage us to explore the significance and meaning of the query and invite further reflection.

Good questions are open-ended in their very nature, and not condemnatory. They can be extended (if yes, why? If no, why not? If I don't know, WHY?), revisited later and revised according to new evidence, perceptions or context. If you are ever tempted to give a slippery, sanitized stock answer response - think, politicians' responses? Probe further.

Responses must be an honest as you dare to be. Useful responses can be yes or no – with justification; a sentence or two or a whole page of outpouring may arise. Sometimes simply considering a

The Real Me

challenging question and noticing that your mind goes quiet can tell you that there's more. And probe further.

You may be familiar with *Plato's Cave* analogy. Let's touch upon it here. Imagine a cave in which prisoners are chained facing a wall, with a fire burning behind them. They have known no other environment. People and animals occasionally move across an outside causeway allowing their shadows to be cast onto the prisoners' wall. The incarcerated folk form judgments about the world outside their cave - their reality - from these shadows, and structure their understanding based on their observations. One prisoner is suddenly released and once in the 'real world' is able to experience these shadows in a different form, matter and material, and to even observe the sun. When she or he returns, excited to tell the others about their misconceptions, the released prisoner is ridiculed and attacked by the others.

Can we consider that all we assume real is perhaps a shadow of the real thing? Could our dearly held truths and beliefs be less than The Real Me?

Caroline Myss states that: "90 percent of our lives is invisible." What might this include?

Our beliefs, our thoughts, our values, and our emotions; our assumptions, wishes, hopes, and dreams, our pain, ideas, inspirations and energy, our wisdom and personality, these are invisible yet very Real aspects of ourselves. Some of these invisible aspects of *Me* are *The Real Me*. Others are not. Many we have absorbed or have been imposed on us and just like mud, they have stuck.

Allow *The Real Me* process to investigate and explore *what is true* and is not deeply true about *Me*, my life, my beliefs and values; what guides my choices, and how I relate to others. Remember, *The*

The Real Me: Not Lost, Just Buried - and Why

Real Me is the fullest expression of you embodying your talents, your passions, your creativity, all the things about you which really make you, *You*; fully alive. Allowing personal, un-examined but accepted falsehoods to be exposed, examined and potentially fall away, gives space for a more balanced, fulfilled, successful You to emerge on all levels, each moment of each day.

The process is NOT about:

- Assuming I'm not enough and trying to engage lifestyle choices to improve *Me*.
- Forcing my square peg into someone else's round hole and - Tada! I'm perfect!
- Being what somebody else wants me to be or what I *think* I should be. Instead consider the concepts that I'm buried and excavating myself – or – I'm scattered to the 4 winds and I'm putting myself back together – or that at some point I stopped listening to *Me*, and now I'm starting again.
- It's also *not* doing whatever I want and engaging in activities which demean or hurt others

Keep in mind that others may prefer a more compliant, controllable you and may not appreciate your inquiry journey and the fruits it may bear. Others may be less excited by your personal discoveries than you expect. The Status Quo is strongly magnetic. Remember also that other people's opinions of you are none of your business!

> "The best day of your life is the one on which you decide your life is your own. No apologies or excuses. No one to lean on, rely on, blame. It's an amazing journey and you will learn you're responsible for the quality of it. This is the day your life really begins."
> (Bob Moawad)

Chapter 2

This Is Me! Feel the Flow

"The difficulty lies not so much in developing new ideas as in escaping from old ones."
(John Maynard Keynes)

How did you find Week 1? What did you notice about yourself and your life as they are now? Relax, and let's spend Week 2 exploring feeling and flow.

This chapter digs deep into our mind's misconceptions of our ego *Me*, what *The Real Me* actually feels like - a beautiful flow - and provides some level 1 tools to come into your *realness* at any moment. Let's use some fresh eyes on *The Real Me*...

Experiencing REAL and Overwhelm

If overwhelm strikes at any point during any of the course, questions, ideas, or material, please stop and hold that space for as long as it is practical for you to do. Be the observer. Gently recognise, allow and accept any feelings of being overwhelmed. Not distracting yourself from how you feel, not judging or escaping. Not forcing yourself to do anything. Noticing how you're feeling in your body and your breath. When you're ready, simply let it go. If you wish, you can return and explore your mental and physical sensations; come back to it, in a few minutes, later today or tomorrow. You can write it down or talk yourself through it. Being able to hold space for unpleasant emotions is an action of The Real Me. No judgement. Use the acronym REAL as below and use the steps in any order which feels right.

Recognise & Relax
Explore & Experiment
Allow & Accept
Let go by non-identification

This is a process we will continue to use throughout the course. You can apply this technique in the grip of difficult emotions as well as positive emotions. As with any skill, it will grow with practise and become habit.

This Is Me! Feel the Flow

You've been gifted a body, including an amazing brain; you've been educated, socialised and created some kind of life for yourself. Yet perhaps you feel or intuit that:

"Some parts of my life are fulfilling, but I feel there's more? Or maybe I want less? I think there are parts of my life where I'm struggling, and not showing up as The Real Me, but I can't quite put a finger on it."

Maybe you read a lot and try new things, but somehow slump back into no-man's land; old habits, living in the fogginess of your rut. Maybe you yearn for elusive Real Me qualities of connection, peace, or freedom (maybe all three?) Perhaps you're okay with *Me* most of the time but occasionally, feel an emptiness that returns, despite a variety of experiences.

Work with this inquiry:

Q: How much of me, and the way I show up, is The Real Me? How much of my current life and lifestyle reflects The Real Me and how much reflects the values of others?

Ask yourself these questions and allow an answer to come up into your understanding. It may be a percentage, an image or some other communication. Mine comes up at around 75% - that's an improvement! When I first wrote this chapter, I was at 52%.

> *"I act like everything is fine. I laugh at people's jokes, I do silly things with my friends and I act like I have a carefree life. It's funny though. When I come back home, I just turn off that mental switch. Then suddenly I break down. I feel alone, empty, tired. It's like I am two different people. One for the public and one for myself. Only if they knew."*
> *(Tanmoy Majumder)*

Let's begin with a move towards accepting where you're at now, with any kind of awareness. Let that awareness begin right now. There are three broad rules of approaching yourself with awareness. Like acceptance, these are simple, but not easy:

1. Grounding *Me* with a simple question: How do I feel in my mind and body right now? Notice any response; words, images, numbers, feelings in your body.

2. Accepting of *MeRightNow* without judgement or wishing it was any different. Tough, right?

3. Understanding that *MeRightNow* is where you are, right now, in this moment. And always will be. This point will change but you will always be where you are *right now*.

Yes, it takes effort to poke and prod at who and why you are, right now. The *"Ouch!"* and *"Oh!"* points are often the most illuminating.

The Real Me Operates in Flow

A big part of *The Real Me* process involves observing yourself. You in Action or Reaction. Simply put, this means *what you choose to do in each moment,* your daily activities and *how you feel* whilst you're doing them.

For the last week, you've been sampling yourself in the midst of many daily activities: *"Why am I doing this? Habit or purpose? If I could really choose, would I be doing this?"* You may have noticed emotions and sensations arise in your body during this process. And you may have noticed some interesting mismatches, especially when something unexpected, an accident or mishap arose. You may have noticed such thoughts as:

"I would never have chosen to put myself in this situation but something about it feels positive. Why? Perhaps because I was able to help someone, or it was really cool to be focused on solving that problem together with others, or just for a moment, it felt good being Me completely immersed in that task."

Alternatively, you may have been doing an activity you actually chose, or taking a well-earned break, then found yourself becoming bored, disconnected or lonely.

Or you may have noticed yourself becoming frustrated or angry or judgemental, then through noticing, your response changed somewhat. Let's explore how feelings, our mismatches and mental judgments give us strong clues towards uncovering *The Real Me*.

Revisit: Throughout this process, I want you to feel safe. Challenged, yet not overwhelmed. In the Zone. Focused but relaxed.

This is one of the foundation principles of *The Real Me* course; we'll call this "Flow"; a term coined and first explored by Mihály Csíkszentmihályi when he was growing up in post-WWII Italy.

> *"A state of Flow is being completely involved in an activity for its own sake."*
> *(Mihály Csíkszentmihályi)*

When you're in a state of *Flow*, the ego (sense of *I am* doing this) falls away. Time flies, slows, stops, or becomes irrelevant.

The Real Me

When you're in flow, "Every action, movement, and thought follows inevitably from the previous one. Your whole being is involved, and you're using your skills to the utmost." (Mihály Csíkszentmihályi)

There's an intense (yet not onerous) absorption in whatever you are doing; an excitement balanced with focused relaxation, body and mind fluidly communicating. Some describe is as a kind of trance. Are you recognizing *The Real Me* anywhere in this description, and perhaps bringing to mind a time when you have experienced *flow*?

What flow is NOT:

- A slumpy feeling of dullness or automatic pilot as you complete a familiar task by rote.

- At the opposite end of the scale; super excited and mentally jumping from one element of the task to another.

- The Grind of doing a task, though you may notice periods of flow within the grind.

Noted author Stephen Kotler says that "Flow is a happy accident, all we can do is become more accident prone." I love this!

Like any skill, flow can be learned and cultivated *with practise.*

We're more likely to experience flow doing an activity which interests us and with a challenge component.

Kotler suggests a 4% challenge above your current skill level; you may or may not resonate with that. To increase your flow-proneness:

- A meaningful (to you) task is more likely to elicit a flow response.

- Turn off or remove distracting devices or elements.

- Mindfulness whilst working the task or experience can expand/deepen into flow.

At its highest level, meditation can drop us into a flow state as our sense of self drops away and there is only the task. This leads me to suspect that flow is itself a spiritual experience but also a continuum with mindfulness at one end and deep meditative ego-release at the other.

The benefits of being in the flow zone at any time during your day will reward you with lowering of blood pressure and slower, subtler breathing which calms your nervous system. Further benefits stretch beyond the experience itself, as increased flow experiences are associated with subjective well-being, satisfaction with life and general happiness. At work, it's linked to productivity, motivation and company loyalty (Stone, A. 2019). Being in flow yourself also inspires others. It's contagious! Here's an example from my own experience.

I was once surprised by an email from my boss asking me to complete a certain time-sensitive task, with which I was unfamiliar, and I suspected would take at least two hours. My boss was away sick and I understood more experienced colleagues would be able to assist. I had a full teaching day and received emails from my boss clarifying certain elements. After school, I gave tutorial assistance to a student and shared mentoring with a colleague. I was then able to begin the two-hour task knowing I'd need to be home in time to put a roast in the oven, as my adult sons were visiting. I needed to scan a heap of student papers, headed over to the library photocopiers and the library was shut. My backup colleagues had left. Catching my drift here?

I had been researching and writing parts of this chapter and throughout this particular experience, I was observing myself through this day. Would I choose to do this? Well...no. Could I simply leave it for colleagues to sort tomorrow? It would be tight and inconvenient for them, but yes, I could bail. Will I have one more go at this?

I asked the question and *The Real Me* decided. Yes.

I headed to the office and was confronted with a state-of the-art photocopying device which said a resolute *"no"* to me doing any scanning. I knew full well that a previous version of *Me* would have been in the grip of rising panic at this point, nonetheless, I took a deep breath and asked for help.

Luckily, one of our beautiful teacher aides (thanks Kathy!) approached, bag in hand, about to leave and said: *"I'll help."*

Instantly, with her expertise it became a one-hour task; not only did she guide me on how to work the petulant machine, she stayed to help me. We completed the task together in a connected kind of flow and I left feeling light and happy.

Dinner was a bit late, but I was completely aware that some of my stubborn, habitual *Me* had been observed, and had fallen away through that process. The whingy *"I can't believe I have to do this with no notice, poor me!"* cultural habitual Me was around but I didn't engage. The mental *"I don't know what to do, I can't do it!"* intellectual habitual Me was left on the sidelines. The panicky

This Is Me! Feel the Flow

"everything's going wrong, I'll let everyone down!" habitual Me was there, just in case I shrieked, but I didn't!

I had engaged in each activity and lesson during that day with fullness, not worrying about the scary monster task waiting for me. I took a lunchbreak, ate and helped the eco club out at lunch. Somehow, the whole day felt flowing and felt good. *The Real Me* was finally present.

This experience at work I consider to be at the mindfulness end of the flow continuum. I have had experiences writing this book where I've looked up at the clock; 4pm, then looked up again, 6pm. Life, kids & cat were going on around me and perhaps this is more authentic mid-range flow. So let's consider flowstate an experience to look out for in daily life and a method to reconnect with the Real Me, as well as an experience to give us clues as to our particular life purpose.

Q: *When* or *doing what activities* do I most often experience a flowstate?

Artists and musicians have been studied in the flowstate but I believe it's available to each of us to explore. And it doesn't have to be the realm of culturally highbrow activities. What about playing your favourite video game? When you're having a wonderful time with great friends? Hiking in nature, baking, or playing cards?

During this week, recognise times, activities, moments where you find yourself in flow state. You might not be sure and this doesn't matter; we're exploring. Explore these moments whilst you're driving, writing, cooking, playing or listening to music, running or exercising, playing a game, creating something, reading, or simply doing a repetitive, yet soothing task.

Chapter 2 Task 1

Key Inquiry Questions

Q: What activity/activities am I doing when I notice myself maybe in a mindful state <-> flowstate?
Q: How does it feel in my body when I am in flowstate?
Q: Am I setting an intention to come into flow, or do I simply find myself there?
Q: For what estimated time periods am I in flowstate each or any day?
Q: Can I describe my mood or feeling of well-being when I notice myself in flow? After I've come out of a flowstate?

If your immediate reaction is that you're rarely in flow state,

- Do you ever daydream yourself into "no mind"?
- Notice moments/activities when you're definitely NOT in flow and write them down.
- Notice moments when you might be in a flowstate, even for a few seconds. Reflect and revisit the Inquiry **Q**.
- Notice other times when you may be on the cusp of flow and it may be a matter of allowing yourself the focus, time and attention to move into a deeper flow-state.

"Intention, attention, no tension. When you're in flowstate your mind (attention) and body is focused and alert but not tense. You may feel some tension before you begin your day, or activity, but find mid flow that your body feels little tension with no tension/anxiety in your mind."
(Marcie Shimoff)

This week, be on the lookout for flowstate in whichever activities you may be engaged.

The Real Me is not my thoughts

Let's chat a bit about tuning in to *feeling* and the separation between feelings, emotions and thoughts.

Western and modern culture teach us the old chestnut: *"I think, therefore I am."* (Descartes)

Our schools place high value on thinking skills and synthesizing new ideas into understanding and skill sets. If you are able to do this quickly, you might be labeled 'clever' or 'smart'; if not, perhaps a 'slow learner' or other, less kind adjectives. If this labeling has ever been applied to you, is this part of *MeRightNow* that you might want to investigate? *The Real Me* doesn't identify with unkind labels. Recognise, Explore, Accept and Let it go. Acceptance is about being open to how an experience made you feel, not accepting it as truth.

I once taught an inspiring Italian exchange student who not only topped my physics class but also topped English as a subject. As English was her second language, this was quite astounding. She said to me that she was very grateful and humble that she was able to learn and integrate new ideas and concepts so quickly. Wow. On the flipside, I feel for people who are more specialized in their learning areas or have struggled with the school system who consider themselves 'not smart' or 'can't learn.' These are *thoughts*; thoughts are not truth and most certainly not *The Real Me*. The Real Me works kindness into every aspect of our lives and particularly treats *ourselves* with kindness. Unkind thoughts are not The Real Me. Not ever.

The Real Me

Thoughts are a crazy person monologue you have with yourself.

Q: What does The Real Me have to say about *that* (any) thought?

Throughout our lives up to now, we have learned to identify with our thinking. We listen to our thoughts. We listen to the judgments, ear-worm songs and scattered streams of consciousness rattling around our heads and on some level, *we believe that **they** are us*. We believe that our mind and that our thoughts/habits/personality make up who we are. In doing so, we have developed the unfortunate *habit of believing what we think*. And often we don't question from where those belief systems and thoughts originated. Remember, we're going to question everything, including - and especially - our most deeply held values and beliefs. This week, whilst working with flow, we will interrogate both our thoughts and belief systems.

So, here comes the brain: our mental hardware and how our brain and body thinks and feels.

Neuroscience 101: Your Brain Is Not Your Mind, But Your Body Might Be

Your *brain* is a physical entity and is the coordinator of all that happens in your body. Your *mind* is a combination of the way your brain functions but also of your experiences and your consciousness. Your mind is your interactive software. And because your brain and sensory organs are made of organic material; your experiences will then feed into your brain - and body - to store.

Your brain's brief is to be a learning device, predominantly to keep you alive. It learns and adapts over time, survival being the number one priority. If an uncomfortable event happens once and perhaps again, then either in reality, or in your perception, it forms habits and then, belief systems. You burn yourself on the hotplate; you immediately learn *"hot"* and *"owww!"* and *"what happened?"* - and some basic first aid! And you learn that danger is real and to be wary.

However, these habits and beliefs were not originally part of your brain, they are learned via your mind, body and experiences, then analyzed and stored as part of your brain/body. We know that our brain is not static; we can entrench neural and physical pathways by continuous use (habits) and diminish them through non-use and non-attention. We also know of neuroplasticity, that we can change our brain function through changing our diet, sleep, habits, attention and emotions.

More on habits: You are not born with a love or hate of pizza, fear of large black dogs or a caffeine addiction neural superhighway! These experiences have been learned; processed by your brain & formed & updated a kind of mental algorithm or mental 'software' over time. Your mind does this by *using your previous software and experiences.*

Thoughts aren't the Real Me

> *"If you realized how powerful your thoughts are you'd never think a negative thought again."*
> *(Peace Pilgrim)*

By now, some of these mental software patterns have become so ingrained, they are now firmware. We firm them by paying attention to them and repeating them. In simplest terms, these thoughts have become regular visitors – habitual thoughts. Swami Jasraj Puri calls them "a committee." Through this course, take time to listen to your thoughts; your committee. Really listen. Are they a friendly, supportive bunch? Notice when they are. *Particularly notice when they are not.*

Regular activities, beliefs or thought patterns & habits (of body or mind) can *change parts of your brain* by strengthening or diminishing particular neural pathways. Some of your committee members are likely not friendly, not serving you and are due for retirement. How do you kick them to the kerb?

Let's engage The *REAL* acronym again. Recognise thoughts, Explore, Accept that they're present (note, this doesn't mean we accept them as truth) don't engage, then action them falling away; Letting go. Bye!

REAL: Recognise, Explore, Accept, Let go with an exhale or a sigh.

Personally, when I recognise my least Real committee members piping up with 'No-one likes me,' and 'I just don't have time,' I take a breath, Relax and explore. I wonder why this thought has come up. Why now? Is there a trigger? Accept and allow the thought to hang; release any engagement emotionally and let go by lengthening my breathing. I accept the thought as not Real and bring myself into the present moment by feeling into my body; feeling my feet on the ground or place my hands on something, then noticing an object in my surroundings that I particularly like; a plant or a cup. It's not distraction; it's a grounding process.

Sometimes I'll explore what triggered the thought in this moment, sometimes not. Examining and exploring is great inner work when you're relaxed and open but can also be a rabbit hole. It's not always appropriate when you're at work, have a deadline looming or someone's in your face. Pick your times and come back to it. You can also extend your Explore **Q** further when confronted by an unwelcome, contracting or unsettling thought.

Key Inquiry Questions

Q: Is it true?
Q: How did I learn this?/Why did this come up for me?
Q: What evidence is there that it's not *The Real Me*?
Q: How does it make me feel?
Q: Have I inherited someone else's suffering?
Q: Do I consider that I can let go and dismantle this over time?
(Developed and extended from Byron Katie's, *The Work*)

Finding release from your most haranguing, heavy, and persistent *Not Me* thoughts can be the most illuminating and authenticating part of this process. Noticing and allowing the *Not Real Me* baggage to fall away. Excavating *The Real Me* will bring incredible mental and emotional freedom and lightness to your interactions with others and simplicity to your life.

Remember, habits are persistent behaviours which derive from persistent thoughts which may not be *The Real Me*. Good habits make you feel open, strong, and Real. Poor habits have historically been outsourced to a support team which is dodgy and dysfunctional. Keep Recognising, Exploring, Accepting and Letting go of what isn't really you and never was.

Personality

Over time, habitual thinking patterns and reactions become labelled as your 'personality.' Is your personality *The Real Me*? Not in its entirety. Remember, habitual behaviours, thoughts, and beliefs can fall away or change with Recognition, Exploring, Allowing, and Letting go, or a particularly strong experience.

The Real Me

"Personality refers to individual differences in characteristic patterns of thinking, feeling and behaving."
(APA, 2019)

It is a broad definition, and personalities are developed and refined over time and by choices and habits, with more or less of *The Real Me* filtering through, depending on your experiences and more particularly, your perceptions of those experiences.

Q: How would I describe my personality to another?
Q: How much of my personality is *The Real MeRightNow*? (Number or %)
Q: How much of my personality is innate and not sculpted by experience or perception?
Q: Which elements of my personality are or are not *The Real Me*?
Q: Which animal, plant or flower might resonate with my personality?
Q: How might a close respected, honest friend describe my personality? (You could even ask them)

Seriously, choose three or four adjectives which might describe your personality right now.

I would describe myself as adventurous, caring, wilful, sociable, creative, vain (sometimes), and as someone who enjoys novelty and new things. And a bit scatty. My husband describes me as lovable, positive and someone who sees the best in people. In Jane Austen's *Pride and Prejudice*, Mr Darcy describes himself as, "Resentful. My good opinion, once lost is lost forever." Personality can be many faceted and variable.

In the eighties, McCrae et al developed a 'Big Five Model' for personality and it is still considered useful and simple today. You can plot yourself along the axis of these five personality traits which research has suggested carries no gender or culture bias.

It is estimated that up to 50% of your current personality is hereditary; I say current, as we know through neuroplasticity that we can change our thoughts, change our habits and thus, our personality.

Chapter 2 Task 2

Date your plot and return to it at the end of this course and examine any differences. Some of the terms are unfashionable in meaning (who would define themselves as neurotic?) Definitions of the 10 terms are below the chart.

Date _____ Date (round 2) _____
Date (round 3) _____

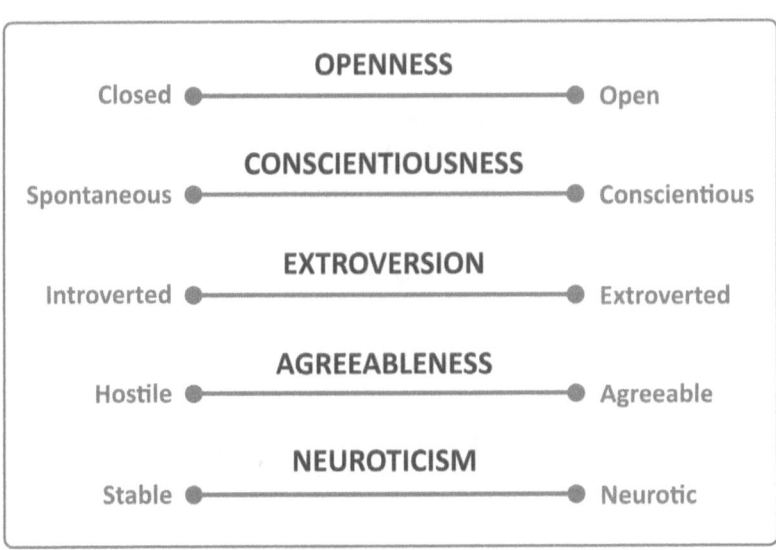

The Real Me

Any surprises here? Ask a family member or friend to take the Big 5 personality assessment and to also rate you. Interesting. Remember, this is simply a tool to explore.

In the last couple of years, we've been teaching this Personality profile to Grade 9 students in school and once students understand the terms, they tend to self-report quite accurately (according to how I would describe them as well as their friends). Some of the terms, like Closed, Hostile and Neurotic are somewhat old-fashioned and have can be viewed as having a negative bias, to the point where a person may resist identifying themselves with these descriptions! I like Crowe Associates (UK) definitions of:

> Openness to experience – (inventive/curious vs. consistent/cautious). Appreciation for art, emotion, adventure, unusual ideas, curiosity, and variety of experience.
>
> Conscientiousness – (efficient/organized vs. easy-going/careless). A tendency to show self-discipline, act dutifully, and aim for achievement; planned rather than spontaneous behaviour.
>
> Extroversion – (outgoing/energetic vs. solitary/reserved). Energy, positive emotions, urgency, and the tendency to seek stimulation in the company of others.
>
> Agreeableness – (friendly/compassionate vs. cool/reserved). A tendency to be compassionate and cooperative rather than suspicious and antagonistic towards others.
>
> Neuroticism – (sensitive/nervous vs. secure/confident). A tendency to experience unpleasant emotions easily, such as anger, anxiety, depression, or vulnerability.

This Is Me! Feel the Flow

I tend towards the Open, Spontaneous, Ambivert (sometimes extroverted sometimes introverted), Agreeable and Neurotic parts of the spectra. My husband is Closed, Conscientious, Introverted, Hostile and Stable. Maybe opposites do attract!

Q: Do I think my preliminary data on the Big Five test shows elements of The Real Me?

Interestingly, some 'personality types' tend to experience the flowstate more regularly. Have a guess which ones. (See end of chapter for answer.)

Nothing Original Here

Your mind, in conjunction with your brain, body and with your experiences does the following:

- **Thinks**
- **Remembers**
- **Analyses**
- **Judges**
- **Justifies**
- **Plans**
- **Sequences**
- **Learns**
- **Recognises**
- **Develops**
- **Uses language**
- **Develops habits**
- **Perceives and filters out what *you tell it (via your attention)* is background information (!!)**

The Real Me

This is a list of vital and useful functions. Much of the 90% of our invisible lives are found here. But there are super-important elements of *The Real Me* missing. Creativity, love, compassion, values, inspiration, inquiry, intuition, dreaming. Our mind is a great tool in service of *The Real Me*.

But what if the mind thinks it **is** *The Real Me* and starts telling us what to do?

Let's consider the nature of our mind as being a wonderful servant, but a terrible master. This is a Buddhist idea which Robin Sharma uses in his book 'The Monk Who Sold His Ferrari'. Sharma reminds us to continually pay attention, and not let our bean-counter of a mind call the shots. Engage it when you need to plan, do a sum or make a list. It can analyse but not evaluate. All our most important decisions are made with our hearts not with our minds. And I like to consider our hearts, both physical and metaphysical, the seat of *The Real Me*.

Defining the mind

Definitions of the mind are numerous and, even within psychology, there is conjecture. According to cognitive psychologist, Steven Pinker, *"The mind is what the brain does."* If so, your mind is not capable of an original thought. *Every thought then is a mishmash of past thoughts, memories, analyses, judgments and habits.* B. F. Skinner retorts that "surely the rest of the body plays a part." Philosopher, Bob Doyle, states that "the mind" refers to the information instantiated within and processed by the nervous system.

In light of no agreed definition of mind, even amongst experts, consider this: anything you think; songs and sentences you hear running about in your head; perhaps they come from permutations of thoughts you've thought before, things you've been told and accepted, shadow beliefs by parents or other significant folk or perhaps something you've read or stumbled upon. It might be something 'new', but you've processed it, thought about it, linked it to what you already know, and it becomes part of what's already there.

> *Thoughts are a whole heap of the past, masquerading as the present, and sometimes the future.*
> *(Idea adapted from Alan Watts)*

Our thoughts are not real and absolutely not the truth. They are created by your mind from experiences (past) and the way your previous and current experiences interact, and also the judgments you make about those experiences.

What about our consciousness?

Those flashes of inspiration, intuition and ideas; the ones that seem to come from nowhere. That's our consciousness in its truest form. *Mary Poppins* author, Pamela Travers, recounts that her main character simply dropped into her head, as does JK Rowling regarding Harry Potter.

Consider this: In moments when we are able to quiet the ever-busy mind, conscious awareness may well be the author of such moments of clarity. It is possible they are actually coming up/down from or expanding out from *The Real Me?*

In her 2009 Ted talk, Elizabeth Gilbert (Eat, Pray, Love) spoke of beliefs in ancient Rome of a genie who lives in our walls and feeds us our ideas, imagination and insights. "The Romans did not actually think that a 'genius' was a particularly clever individual. They believed that a genius was this, sort of magical divine entity, who was believed to literally live in the walls of an artist's studio, rather like Dobby the house elf, and who would come out and sort of invisibly assist the artist with their work and would shape the outcome of that work". The same scenario can happen with emotional triggers. If you don't have *that* thought, hear *that* song or experience *that* smell then no response.

What does a response typically look like? Physiologically, parts of your brain are activated – brain stem (reptile brain), amygdala and hypothalamus. Facial expressions and behaviours suddenly change. Hormones and chemicals are released into your blood, causing heart rate and breathing alterations. We have distinct physical and physiological responses or reactions to that which we might call an emotion. Interestingly again, if your aroused emotional state comes from a thought, *a simple thought*; signals are shot from the memory centres first, *then* amygdala, hippocampus and neocortex.

Emotions and Feelings, Mind and Body

During any day, you will notice emotions arising then over time, returning to some kind of normal, baseline or origin. Like a Sine or ocean wave, coming back to a steady mid Origin point. E-motions are Energy in Motion and can flood your being with happiness, sadness, anger, fear, surprise, disgust, and so on.

Emotion Sine wave

The Origin point in the Sine wave diagram is your relaxed, alert, conscious state of being. You in general Flow. The amplitude is the strength of your emotion, the period (time taken for one complete wave, not shown) is how long the departure from your Origin lasts and the wavelength is the space between such events.

This Is Me! Feel the Flow

This analogy may not work for everyone but perhaps 'seeing' a sine wave flash before your eyes as an emotional escalation is occurring may enable you to step back from it and reduce the amplitude. Maybe you enjoy the big highs but struggle with the lows. Perhaps the analogy will assist you coming back to calm and balance more quickly as you know what's happening. You can set an an intention to reduce the Period and come back to gentle flow, your normality point; your settled Origin. This is *The Real Me*.

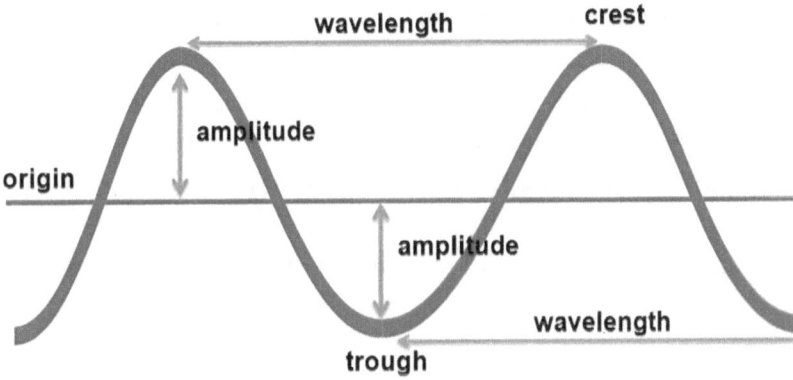

These fluctuations of emotion come quite quickly; often with little warning and we find ourselves not in control. This can be fine if we're celebrating a big win with our team, less so when we burst into tears at work or find ourselves yelling at someone. Sometimes the emotions will leave quite quickly, and other times they'll stick around. Especially if you are in the habit of nursing them, re-hashing and mentally returning to them. Either way, at some point your emotion will subside and you'll notice your central *normality* point from which your emotions vacillate.

The Real Me

Assignment for Chapter 2

Task 1: Be aware of your thoughts and emotions today or tomorrow; living your life, notice the happy and the sad moments; the supportive and unsupportive thoughts. A little happy, a little sad. Notice your own personal Sine wave.

You might be in traffic and noticing your mind wandering to a worry or concern, and you're just a little bit miserable; Maybe you woke feeling unusually sunny, you've had a really great run in to work or you've just stepped outside and seen the most amazing group of birds flying, and you feel that immediate sense of: *"Ahhh!"*. And maybe a bit later, you spill your coffee on your lap and: *"Ugh!"*, just like that you're sad. Now you notice; happy, sad, happy, sad.

And notice when you're in your Origin, the normality point of relaxed flow, from where your emotion or mood may seem to go up and down from like a wave; these are the sorts of vacillations to notice today.

Emotions stem from your mind interacting with experiences and thoughts during your day.

Emotions Inquiry Q

Q: Identify an event or person or comment which might cause/trigger a ten (top amplitude) on my personal emotional Sine wave.
Q: What's my general daily Amplitude? +5 to -5 , +1 to -1 ? What would I like it to be?
Q: Consider the Period of my wave. Short or long. How might I bring myself back to Origin in a more timely manner?

This Is Me! Feel the Flow

Feelings

Feelings on the other hand, are embodied experiences; ie, involve your body.

When we talk about feelings we're talking about the felt experience. Emotions may begin with a thought or external event but become feelings when the emotion becomes a whole-body experience.

My own personal definition of feelings vs emotion is that *Feelings are embodied, deep and positive*, reflecting the universal truths of love, joy, and peace. Of course there are simple, immediate feelings like hunger, pain and tickles!

Think for a moment within your own experiences about how joy is different to happiness. Joy is a deep sense of *The Real Me* and we're going to tap into that. And while we will go through the daily happy, sad, happy, sad states, the really deep sense of joy is always with you. It's always there. If you step inside, beyond the thought experiences of any given moment and into your deepest truths:

You're joyful about being alive.

You're joyful about having meaningful connections with others.

You're joyful about the opportunity to have incredible experiences.

You're joyful about who you are, confusing as it may be.

Consider your family; they cause you moments of annoyance, and grief, and upset, and delight, but there's a deep joy that they're in your life.

The Real Me

The depth and breadth of those really deep positive Feelings are the foundations of *The Real Me*. Joy, love, and you might want to include peace with that. That might get you thinking, "Love, joy, and Peace, that sounds like a Christmas card or spiritual text." I believe there's a real connection here because The Real Me is tapping back into your spirit and connecting *you* back into you. The spirit of You is who you really are.

> *"I discovered that when I believed my thoughts, I suffered, but that when I didn't believe them, I didn't suffer, and that this is true for every human being. Freedom is as simple as that. I found that suffering is optional. I found a joy within me that has never disappeared, not for a single moment. That joy is in everyone, always."*
> *(Byron Katie)*

I know Week 2 has been a BIG week. Relax, connect with yourself and work at your own pace. Your perceptions and understandings of thought, emotions and feeling may be different to mine and that's brilliant; we're exploring.

Continue to work through your assignment for Week 2, paying attention to thoughts, feelings and emotions this week. Envision your Sine wave of emotions during each day. Moreover, note periods you've maybe experienced flow, what you were doing and how it felt in your mind and body.

Keep noting down persistent thoughts and emotions to consider. *The Real Me?*

Chat to others about their perception of your Personality and note your own descriptions of yourself.

This Is Me! Feel the Flow

Note:

What have you learnt about *The Real Me?*

What habits have you noticed and are considering letting go?

Chapter 3

The Real Me, Naked and Now

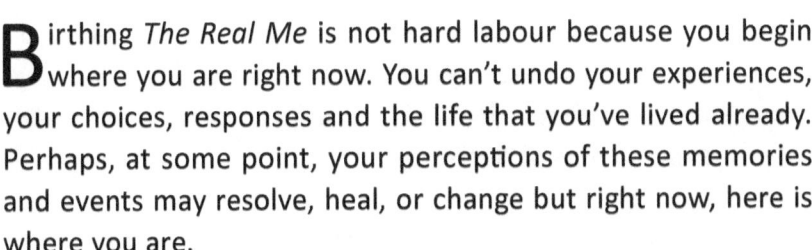

Birthing *The Real Me* is not hard labour because you begin where you are right now. You can't undo your experiences, your choices, responses and the life that you've lived already. Perhaps, at some point, your perceptions of these memories and events may resolve, heal, or change but right now, here is where you are.

The really tough challenges you've experience have altered your perceptions of life and of yourself already, and through it all, you've developed some crusty armour around some of the most creative, sensitive and *Real Me*-shaped parts of you. This happens because our minds work very hard to give us an *identity* based on previous experiences. And there is no way to be *Me* without having these lived experiences, nor can we re-invent or imagine *Me* in a state of blissful, ignorance, even if we could somehow delete or lobotomize our most painful and difficult memories.

These experiences and our interpretation of them have changed not only our lives but also our bodies. Science, genetics and psychology have come a long way in the last fifty years and we now know that:

- Our genes and basic DNA are not a fixed library. The study of our DNA plasticity is called epigenetics. Our experiences, trauma, thoughts, habits and diet can radically change our genetics – for better, or for worse.

- Neuroplasticity. We know that we can re-wire our brains; not simply after a brain injury, but anytime we like. We can change our attention, change our thoughts, change our habits, and ultimately, change our lives.

- Our mind, body and energy are all connected and are constantly chatting to each other. Often our mind, especially if it has been allowed to form deep negative ruts or run rogue, often does most of the talking. Especially if we have busy jobs, family demands, stressful lives and beyond-high expectations of ourselves.

Our choices change our hormone balances, which further alter our physical bodies and mental states. Research from hundreds of studies have shown links between the stress hormone, cortisol, and a variety of physical conditions from sleep issues, carrying excess weight, to slow healing. None of these and other conditions are *The Real Me*.

The Real Me is healthy, balanced, and in flow.

The Real Me, Naked and Now

Other people's ideas, their version of you, judgement of yourself by yourself and others, the personality traits you've developed and the way that you have engaged rules for your own life are all congealed into *MeRightNow*. And much of this armour is not *The Real You*.

Other people's traumas and mud-slinging that has been allowed to stick and harden; gas-lighting, misunderstandings, burdens you weren't equipped to shoulder, hurts done to you and by you; your own personal traumas all contribute to *MeRightNow*. None of this is *The Real You* but it has been absorbed by you. Into you. And we want to release it.

We will inquire, explore and unburden *The Real Me and* we'll do this moment to moment. You simply can't do it wrong. The results are pure liberation.

Getting To Know *MeRightNow*

Continuing our work from Weeks 1 & 2, we're going to sharpen our powers of observation. Learn to Pay Attention. It's a project, and you're it. The part of you that's the observer - some people like to call it your higher Self, or your super-ego, your conscience, Jiminy Cricket or the angel on your shoulder - is going to observe. For the last two weeks, we've been paying a bit more attention to all sorts of things in our lives; noticing what we find ourselves *doing* and our choices; paying attention to moments of flow, as well as thoughts emotions as they arise. Noticing. Feeling. Whilst you've been undertaking these processes, you've been evoking and practicing the art of self-observation; of paying attention. Here's the crux of living life as *The Real Me* in one sentence:

The Real Me

In each and every moment of your life, your task is to pay attention.

The beauty and apparent ease of *The Real Me* method is that, in effect, you are not *doing* anything different. No checklist of difficult changes to somehow make or add in an over-full life.

Continue living your life the way you do, not necessarily deliberately changing anything.

But now you are really looking at what's right in front of you, rather than gazing past it; really listening to what's happening around you, to you, rather than being in greyness. Listening with your whole being when someone speaks to you, listening to yourself, listening to the words that come out of your mouth. Your opportunity is to engage any and each of your five senses in any given moment.

You are watching with new eyes, listening with new ears, as well as paying attention to information coming in through your other senses. Sensations of warm & cool, clothing and jewellery against your skin, a lingering scent in the air or savouring the taste of food or drink, rather than sipping or shovelling food into your body whilst working.

Most importantly, as you are the observer, you are *noticing* but *not engaging with* any negative mental dialogue about your current experience, which may sound something like:

"Oh, this coffee is too cold, he never makes it right!" or, "She hasn't said 'good morning', what have I done wrong?"

Notice any habitual negative judgments with a sense of, *"Oh, how interesting that came up; is that The Real Me?"* Ask yourself this question. Over and over again. *'Is this the Real Me??'*

Three Guidelines of Paying Attention

1. Notice physical elements of your experience right now. Feelings.
   Ask yourself: What am I observing with my senses? What am I feeling in my body?
2. Notice thoughts as they arise.
   Enjoy the positive thoughts, how do they feel in my body? Notice the negative thoughts, how do they feel? Notice the neutral thoughts. Recognise, Examine, Accept, Let go. Then simply let them go and come back to being in the present moment.
3. Allow no judgments of whatever should be happening right now. It is what it is.
   If I'm tempted to judge, can I reframe it, interrogate it or simply let it go and come back to now?

Exercise 1: Being MeRightNow

Allow one minute for this exercise.

Centre your awareness at your feet - or choose a different body part; hands, belly or hips. What's happening there right now? Footwear/clothes or none? Narrow your awareness to one foot (or chosen body part), then to parts of that foot, then the toes. Hello toes! Hold your awareness there for three breaths, following the guidelines 1-3 above.

What are your toes feeling like; are they cosy, warm or cool? Are they cramped or free? Any pain or discomfort? Do you notice yourself moving and wiggling them as your attention is foot-centred? Allow them to relax, then shift your attention to something

The Real Me

outside of your body, perhaps outside the window? in your room? Just in front of you? Hold your awareness there for three breaths. Now bring awareness back to reading the text.

And that's just it - there are *so many* things to which we could possibly pay attention in any given moment. When you first start to do this, it can drive you a little crazy. There are *so* many things to which you can pay attention. *So many things*, everything, and it suddenly becomes overwhelming. And the reason that we often retreat from *The Real Me* is because to be in touch, in tune, connected with everything that's physically us *and* that's occurring around us at every moment, can feel incredibly exhausting. Is it even possible? Of course not.

An accepted figure in neuroscience is that our brains can process *eleven million bits* of information every second, but we can only consciously pay attention to between twelve and fifty bits. Wu et al found that this number decreases to 1-6 bits for higher order tasks. (Personally, it seems like I can only process around six bits most of the time!). The vast majority of information coming into our senses is processed completely outside our conscious awareness.

Exercise 2: Greying Out

'Greying out' is my term for your mind muscling into your present moment, distracting you with memories, plans, judgments, or any random thought not related to *MeRightNow*.

A random thought will turn into a story, perhaps rehashing an emotional event, memory, plan or daydream and you suddenly find yourself somewhere far, far away. Greying out is *all* mind based. You remember things past, and find yourself not interacting with the present or showing up as *The Real Me*. You can also grey out by worrying about the future, as well as when you attempt to multitask. (How can you really savour a delicious apple whilst typing, conversing and kicking off a shoe at the same time?)

Are you regularly forgetting where you put your keys/glasses/phone/anything? Your mind has moved on whilst you were using or putting down this item. Not in the present moment.

Our minds generally want to escape the present moment as it's incredibly exhausting and intense. So we grey out. We daydream. We think ourselves somewhere else.

Work with the following flow exercise for a few moments; extend it for as long as you are able. And don't worry, you can't do it wrong. Remember, to re-discover *The Real Me*, it will take some time and practice to get to know yourself. The simplest exercises and questions can be the most transformative as you are not putting yourself under pressure or trying to *measure up*, and they don't invite judgment.

This is a breathing and grounding exercise:

- As you read, notice your next breath. Inhale, and exhale.
- Inhale again and notice physical sensations - your chest and belly move, you feel movement of air in your nostrils, maybe even on your upper lip. I usually notice the gentle thud of my heart beating and sometimes, some tension in my shoulders. You may also notice your posture, feel your sitting-bones on the seat, sofa or bed and where you can, sit a little straighter.
- Now prepare to do the same exercise again, this time with your eyes closed. Read ahead so you know when to stop.
- Close your eyes and notice your next inhale, then your next exhale, then your next inhale, and continue. Stop when

you find your mind wandering from the task at hand; when you notice a thought (usually) or a sensation which is not related to the task you've set yourself; the task is simply noticing your breathing and body sensations. Any idea or thought, qualifies as a Stop.
- Restart.
- Using an affirmation or a simple mental statement like: *"I am breathing in"* or "I am wonderful" during the inhale, and *"I am breathing out" or "I am relaxing"* on the exhale, can extend your attention on your breathing task. Essentially, it gives the busy mind a job to do. It does split some of your attention from noticing the breath alone; nevertheless, notice.
- Close your eyes and practice again using the mental statement, or an affirmation of your own. Stop when your mind wanders again, or you find yourself greying out.
- When you've completed, or decided you've had enough, consider:

Q: How does my body feel now? My mind? What did I notice?
Q: Do I *feel* more grounded? More calm? More Real?
We know our mind meanders and jumps around a lot; it's often called the *'monkey-mind.'* It can be slippery, mischievous and all over the place. There's no prize for honing your attention for minutes at a time, and no judgment when finding yourself greying out in a second or three. We're getting to know *MeRightNow.* This is a great exercise to practice daily and watch your ability to stay *with* yourself, *as* yourself in a relaxed state of flow, increase from moments to minutes. This practice is grounding yourself in *The Real Me.*

Be aware that we probably notice it more when other people grey out, than when we do it ourselves. And we *do* notice it when we're talking to somebody, they glaze over and seem to drift away for a little bit, and it hits you that this person is really not with you in that moment.

Often, we'll make judgments as to whether we're being boring or whether something else is happening with them. Of course, it's likely a habit they've developed over a lifetime. Do you do it too? Notice. Conversely, you also notice when someone's attention never waivers when they are with you; they are really with you and seem to *come alive,* just because you are in their presence. It feels amazing and perhaps a little confronting to be with such an intense individual; it's *The Real Me* and it's contagious!

This week, notice when *You* start to grey out, when your mind wanders from the present moment. Some of our most fruitful and difficult attention-paying moments are when we're in conversations with others, and we find ourselves considering what we are going to say next, rather than really listening to their words, receiving their body language, and other subtexts during interaction. Or when we are reading the same sentence five times without engaging, our mind keeps wandering elsewhere. Or when you trip, stumble or walk into something or someone because rather than tuning into your footsteps and the day around you, your mind has dragged you into a *Not-Now* thought.

Assignment for Chapter 3

*Notice when your mind bolts, retreats or just drops away from your present moment. Notice **where** your mind wanders. Notice how your monkey mind might interrupt anytime you are in flow.*

You may start to notice common triggers that draw you away from paying attention, being in flow and the NOW:

There is always a choice.

The Real Me

Choosing to stay in flow or return to flow or refocusing on the present moment when we grey out is a choice, always available to us.

Attention, flow and pulling ourselves out of the grey and back into the RightNow (with all its difficulties) with awareness IS the choice to be The Real Me, in every moment.

Trial these exercises this week:

1. Notice when your attention and awareness wander from whatever you are doing or saying Right Now.
2. When you notice yourself greying out, practice repeating to yourself, "I am The Real Me, I am here; I am The Real Me, I am here," and keep coming back to yourself, RightNow. If this phrase seems stilted and doesn't appeal, formulate your own; use your name or codeword or number. Use one of the stimuli from No. 3 below to bring yourself back to the Now.
3. Ground yourself back into the present with a particular physical stimulus. Pick any one of these examples:
    - I feel my feet on the floor
    - I notice my breath
    - I feel myself holding this pen
    - I feel my tongue on the roof of my mouth
    - I feel I've just blinked
    - _____
    _____
    _____
    (space for your own idea)
4. Practice, practice, practice.

The Real Me, Naked and Now

You'll find you'll keep wandering off; greying out and you'll keep coming back. Come back, *The Real Me*, come back. Keep returning to right now. Practice, practice, practice. And then some. Notice who's around you. The colours, sounds, and sensations that you feel on your skin, smells, your tastes, and the things with which you really connect. Notice the things that you don't connect with. We're not judging. We're not saying, *"Oh, that's bad."* But the things that you tend to positively connect with are the things that feed into the real version of you, the authentic *Real Me*.

Inquiry Questions:

This week's questions will start you noticing your particular distractors. Things, people, times of day, objects or thoughts that are part of your personal greying out habits. You have the opportunity to identify - if you chose.

Q: Am I triggered away from paying attention by a particular person or group of people?
Q: Do I procrastinate about paying attention and resist getting into flow, particularly if I'm facing a challenging task?
Q: Is there a decidedly well-travelled mental loop (rut), usually negative, that I find myself dropping into? eg *"I'm no good, I can't do it, people hate me, I always mess up, what's the use?"*
Q: Do I find myself feeling bored within the present moment? (Interesting, that one. Explore why?)
Q: Do I start to make judgments when 'nothing's happening'? Or 'there's too much happening!'?
Q: Do I reach for my phone, something to read, a cup of tea when there is no activity, drama or deadline in my *Now*?

The Real Me

Q: In any activity, is there a time frame? For example, can I commit my attention for a minimum of 30 seconds, before I lose focus and grey out?
Q: How do I tell if I've greyed out?
Q: If I choose to return to my flow state, the Now or paying attention, how does it feel in my mind and/or body?
Q: How am I feeling right now?

These are big questions but they will help to return to how you are feeling at any moment.

Below, I've included a more advanced practice and you might find yourself identifying just one or two per day. It's all interesting and an enlightening progress for *The Real Me*:

Q: When I grey out, does a negative thought pattern come up, a doubt? Is this a common thought on 'loop'?
Q: Do I drift into a worry about some future event, or about some future interaction? Is this a common type of thought (although subject might change) on 'loop'?
Q: Do I find myself drifting into journeys, into past grievances or sorrows? How does this feel in my body?
Q: Do I find myself being swept away with an intuitive idea? How does this feel in my body?

Be prepared to really step into feeling, rather than thinking.

Feeling is holistic, as it's our body-mind experiencing our lives and choices. Feeling is exploration, listening and The Real Me. Thinking is judging, ego and old patterning.

Come back to those feelings of lightness, openness, expansion, and we're working *particularly now*, on curiosity. So, when you're noticing what's happening in the moment, when you're noticing sights, sounds, colours, smells, and tastes, and anything else, notice the elements that feel light in your body - they feel open, they feel expanded.

Notice if there are activities, events, words, places or situations with which you connect feelings of openness and lightness; with the sense *of The Real Me*. Conversely, notice events or situations in which you suddenly start to feel contracted, or small, or heavy. This can easily extend to words, as well as places and particular people. *Not me.*

Have you ever had a close relationship with someone - family, friend or colleague - who you find completely draining? If there's such a person in your life now, approach them with interest rather than dread. Notice. You might notice something as simple as just feeling tired, breathless, prickly skin, tension, dry mouth, very heavy, confused or even drowsy. Sometimes it can feel like you've just eaten a big, heavy meal.

Use your journal to jot down some of the experiences that you've had with paying attention, and coming back to the present moment, to what you're experiencing with your senses, and to how that feels in your body. You might like to blog it. Or you might simply like to consider it. Or you don't need to do any of these things. To be effective, The Real Me exercises need to be engaging, yet not onerous. Keep coming back. Noticing. You're starting to get to know yourself from the outside back in, whilst really tuning in to what's happening around you.

How is that making me feel? What's happening on the inside?

Our ego-mind loves routine things; of course! It's constructed by years of your algorithms that will convince you that paying attention right now is really dull - doesn't the mind just hate being surprised? (*The Real Me* loves surprises! Ask yourself why.) And as you're being Present, you'll find yourself drifting into not-Present, perhaps rehashing a conversation that maybe didn't go as you'd hoped, perhaps preparing for a difficult one, yet to occur. Your mind will expertly and covertly grey you into *anything* rather than being right here, *Right Now*, in the present moment. Being in the present moment, is a very strong part of connecting back to *The Real Me*. What you are in this moment, right now, IS *The Real Me*.

Something that happened five minutes ago, last year, even ten years ago, is no longer *Real*.

If you're thinking about a *memory*, you're bringing a *version of what happened back then, into the present moment* while you're thinking about it. If it's a painful experience, a whole load of baggage will come attached, especially if it's come up uninvited.

It's a fantasy, not a memory.

And any future event that you find that yourself planning, worrying and fretting about, even excited about, is NOT *Real*. Again, your thoughts and habits are bringing a version of it into your present; it's capturing your attention with fantasy. What's *RealRightNow* are the sensations you're feeling in your physical body, what you're seeing, what you're noticing, what you're observing, hearing, feeling, tasting, smelling; a conversation you are having *right now*, the words you are reading *right now*, the experience you are having with your body and mind interacting with your surroundings, whatever you choose to alight your attention on, *right now*.

Of course, you can choose to write a shopping list or plan a holiday with reference to a future event. *You* are still writing and planning in the *Now*. You can choose to bring a delightful or even a painful memory into the present and consider elements of it as part of your *Now*. This can be incredibly healing and great chunks of *Not-Me* can fall away when we invite old wounds into the present with compassion. Continue to question everything that you observe in your *Now*.

And another benefit of being in the present is that time slows down. Have you experienced the aphorism that 'a watched pot never boils'? Of course it does, and in the same time it takes if you wander away, but time seems to slow down as you stand and watch it. Even Einstein said time isn't a constant. Consider these ideas.

Now, for some encouragement.

Remember, you're the only one that can do this work. Only you can be the fullest expression of yourself in all your simple, wonderful, creative glory. This is your life's work. Whilst we start stripping away layers of ourselves that aren't really us, we are also building and living an inventory of *who we are*, in both easy and difficult moments. We begin noticing when we platitude instead of converse, noticing feelings in our stomach and body around certain events, and noticing how we behave in a variety of situations. New eyes, new ears and new awareness.

If you find yourself noticing that you don't like elements of what you observe, then you're doing your inquiry practice absolutely right. You're paying attention. As 'the observer' you'll notice different things about you and around you. You'll notice perhaps even some of the choices that you make in the moment.

You will find it exhausting, and you'll find yourself coming back to your chosen grounding practice - and you'll find yourself drifting back into not paying attention. And then you'll come back, come back, come back, and you'll drift off into not paying attention again. Is this Mindfulness practice? Yes it is.

Wherever you are, be there.

> *"Lifestyle is not something we do; it is something we experience. And until we learn to be there, we will never master the art of living well."*
> *(Jim Rohn)*

The only way to do this effectively and keep it Real is to start small. Just keep practicing and bringing yourself back. To RightNow and to where you are. The richness of every moment of our lives is overwhelming, and you will feel tired and out of your comfort zone, just like the naked newborn that you are.

This week, work with exercises 1 & 2 and the assignment questions, enjoy, have fun and flow!

Further Reading

'The Power of Now' (*Eckhart Tolle*)

'Become What You Are' *(Alan Watts)*

Chapter 4

Tools for Embodying The Real Me

We will work with two active tools to gently uncover and expose The Real Me, beginning today. As you might expect, they're solitary pursuits, though you can practice all of them in group settings.

The tools are:

1. Grounded Breathing
2. Meditation

Notice if your ego-mind makes judgments here, before we've even begun!

Lets take a deep, relaxed breath.

The Real Me

Breathing. One word; everybody does it.

We're going to learn how breath awareness together with another simple grounding practice connects you to *The Real Me* and to the present. And remember, we learn and become *The Real Me* by experiencing.

Meditation. It's not scary or boring. You'll learn basic skills and establish a practice.

Each of these tools get you out of your sometimes-subversive mind, and back into *The Real Me* and therefore, back into your Real life.

I love these practices as they enable you to spend time... with yourself.

Simply, MeRightNow and *The Real Me* hanging out and getting to know each other in Real time.

1. Grounded Breathing

A grounded breathing practice can be explored with either your feet or whole body grounded on the floor. Metaphorically speaking, grounding keeps you *down to earth* and anchors you into your feeling body-mind, *The Real Me*.

We'll work with three separate sets of five complete cycles of breaths (a complete breath cycle includes one full inhale and one full exhale) as guided below. This practice usually takes around 3-5 minutes.

Browse through the next two paragraphs and, if not now, commit to a place and time to work through the practice today:

Tools for Embodying The Real Me

Ensure you're sitting comfortably with your back fairly straight, or you can choose to practice grounded breathing laying down, on the floor or the bed is fine. If you are in bed, a straight spine is preferable, so place a full pillow under your knees and a flatter pillow under your head. Familiarize before practicing or have a friend or family member read it to you. Once completed a few times, you will be able to practice from memory each day and allow adjustments to make it your own practise.

1. The Grounded Breathing Practice:

*"When you own your breath,
nobody can steal your peace."*
(Anon, cited by Jess Evelyn)

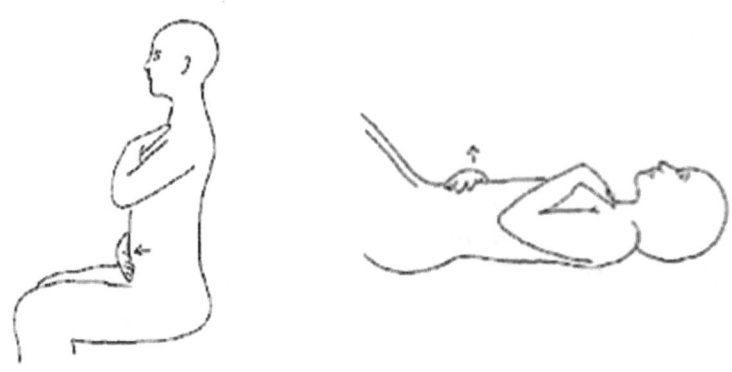

(Thanks to Wellbeing365.com.au for images)

Take a few, normal relaxed breaths, placing your left hand, palm facing down on your belly; and your right hand, palm facing down on your chest, palms loosely opened. Relax your arms then your shoulders; relax your neck, then your face. Finally, relax your hips and legs. Your posture is both relaxed and energized; avoid passive and slumpy. Eyes can be closed or lowered gaze.

The Real Me

Part 1:

For five breaths or five rounds, simply notice your breath. Keep your attention firmly yet gently on your breath and body.

A round is one complete breath in, one complete breath out. And continue for 5 rounds. If you are sitting, make sure your feet are on the floor. This is all about being relaxed and present. Go.

When you've completed, take a few relaxed normal breaths and open your eyes fully. Consider:

Q: How am I feeling (physically, feeling or emotionally)? Choose 3 adjectives.
Q: Did I close my eyes? (It's perfectly fine to close eyes or lower your gaze).
Q: Did I notice my mind wandering away or greying out? (Remember, no judgement).
Q: If so, was I able to bring my attention back to the practice?
Q: Did the length of my breath feel a little longer at the end of the fifth breath than it was at the start, when I was first exploring?
Q: Did I feel my belly, as well as my chest moving?
Q: Did I notice any discomfort and need to change posture? (If so, always take a moment to remedy).

If you have pain, or noticed tension in any part of the body, pay particular attention and imagine your inhaling breath to flow to that body area and with your exhale allowing this body area to relax.

Tools for Embodying The Real Me

Part 2:

Count to four during both inhale and exhale.

When you're ready, we're going to do the same again. Five rounds. This time we're going to mentally *count during the breath.* Most people's count roughly matches their heartbeats. Check your grounding and posture. On the inhale, to count to four and space your counting evenly. Allow each breath to be easy and natural; don't force a longer breath, but allow it as it happens.

1
2
3
4

On the exhale count to four; space your counting evenly.

1
2
3
4

Five rounds. When completed, take a few normal, easy breaths and open your eyes fully. Consider the following:

Q: How am I feeling (physically, feeling or emotionally)?
Q: Did my mind wander/ grey out *less* using the counting grounded breathing?
Q: Did I find towards the end of my exhale that I probably could have extended to a count of five, breathing at the same relaxed rate?
If you prefer, you can re-visit the previous inquiry questions.

Part 3:

Extend the exhale.

For the third round, we're going to continue a **count of four on the inhale and on the exhale, and we're going to extend it to a count of five** or if it's comfortable for you, for a count of six.

Remember, no forcing here; release the ego. It's very easy for your ego to want to increase the count and I'm going to caution you here. First, inhale for four, exhale for five counts of the same pace. And if you really feel it extending easily and *comfortably*, then allow it to extend to six. If, after a couple of breaths, you find breathing to six feels forced and tension builds; somewhat breathless, then roll effortlessly back to a count of 5 on the exhale, or even 4 and a half!

When you're ready, making sure you're nice and comfortable. And again, if it works for you, close your eyes or just lower your gaze. If you're on a bus or a train and you don't want to concern the person next to you too much, then just simply lower your gaze a little and simply focus on your breath. Five breaths. Again, when completed, a few easy, normal breaths, eyes fully open and consider:

Q: What did I observe?
Q: Did I find it pleasant or unpleasant? Calming? Difficult? Or neutral?
Q: Did any particular thoughts come up for me?
Q: Was I able to focus only on my breath?

Did you find your legs hips or spine feeling uncomfortable? Your body feeling heavy and relaxed?

Notice if your lower body feels heavy yet your chest and upper body feel light. You may need to lean forward gently when completed to release tension in your lower back or gently twist your spine or circle shoulders. Allow your body to be the guide. Notice if you feel calmer.

Simply notice.

The neuroscience behind the longer exhale is that it engages the parasympathetic nervous system (PNS); our 'rest & digest' part of the autonomic nervous system. The PNS we've engaged is our birthright modus operandi, our flow and relaxed nervous response and the optimal conditions for our immune & digestive systems as well as healthy new cell creation. Breathing longer & deeper into our bodies and feeling our bellies rise and fall with breath also triggers this response. It's a really clever, simple tool to get back into being *The Real Me,* disconnect with your ego-mind and reconnect with your body-mind.

Allow it to be easy and relaxed.

Assignment for Chapter 4

We're going to do the grounding and breathing practices thrice every day. Once in the morning; when you first wake, or at a time when you might sit to have a break, cuppa tea or those 5 quiet minutes when you've eaten breakfast or lunch, but not quite ready to return to duties. Then again, later in your day; once in the afternoon and once in the evening. Feel free to drop the hands from your belly and chest if you like and allow hands to rest comfortable in your lap or on your thighs, palms up.

It will take a little effort. There might be time when you've just come home and sat down. When I used to drive to work, I'd sit in the car once home and do my grounded breathing before I'd re-enter the fray of family, dinner, marking, teaching Yoga and running kids around. For you, there might even be a time when you're at the gym, walking or doing exercise. It's a quite different scenario when you're exercising. It's quite easy to count the breath if you're running, swimming or walking; make sure you keep your eyes open!

Tune back into how I was feeling a moment ago. Your breath is part of being in your flow state, always in the present moment and connecting you to *The Real Me*. Breath reconnects us to our body, in the present moment. Your breath is like a mirror. When you're relaxed and calm and open, your breath reflects your third round of practice; quite relaxed, easy, and deeply energizing your whole self with no white-knuckle effort. And your exhale can often tend to be a little longer than your inhale. Have you ever noticed what happens when you sigh? Or that long, beautiful exhale when you've finished a task in flow?

The Real Me is always a relaxed *Me*, even when you're fun and excited and doing crazy things. *The Real Me* will always be acting, playing, and working in a relaxed, easy manner, rather than a tense, anxious or nervous manner. Notice.

Part 4: Getting to know your Body

Let's get back to the breath mirroring how you're feeling. Now, we are going to explore *the felt experience.*

The felt experience is noticing sensations in your body. We've been tuning into this already with many of our Questions, such as:

Tools for Embodying The Real Me

How does my body feel? Where in my body do I feel this? Without judgement, how does this feel? Do I need to adjust? How & why?

For those of us who have learnt over many years and experiences to really close off from our bodies, you may only notice a little, and not very often, but every moment of felt awareness is precious, educational and cumulative.

Many of us are used to not listening to our bodies and our felt experiences until something is very wrong, either acute or chronic.

Although I would agree, *"You are not your body"* (Dr B. Weiss), our body anchors us into the present moment. It is always in the present; never the future or the past. That's the ego-mind's domain. So, if we are choosing to show up as *The Real Me*, much of *Me* is here now, in my body.

So, let's learn to notice, pay attention and cherish our bodies; our vehicle for life.

Our body has an intrinsic wisdom of its own and will let us know when our priorities, schedules, diets, sleep and hormones aren't supporting us as a flowing, balanced *Real Me*.

Notice your body. Listen and respond.

Body and breath are connected in that they are *both always in the present* and can haul us out of a worried, anxious or depressed state of mind back into *RightNow* using the grounding practise above or the exercises in Chapter 4. In the *RightNow*, things generally aren't as bad as our tricky mind might have us believe.

The Real Me

The Present Moment, our *Now* can indeed be beautiful. Dreadful experiences from the past aren't happening *Now*, any fantasy or worry about our future isn't happening *Now*. We may find ourselves in an interesting, challenging, engaging, healing flow state, *RightNow*.

> *"Body awareness not only anchors you in the present moment, it is a doorway out of the prison that is the ego. It also strengthens the immune system and the body's ability to heal itself."*
> (Eckhart Tolle)

Exercise: Embrace the Now, exploring your breath!:

Here are some scenarios; when you see a #, feel free to re-enact these breath situations and feel into your own body; for each scenario, take a few moments afterwards to notice what sensations each one evokes. Feel.

We just talked about the sigh. Allow yourself to sigh and Feel your whole body sighing – what does that feel like to you? Do it again.

What happens to your breath when you're crying? It's harsh and stilted, halted and gaspy. Chest breaths. Trial it and feel.

What happens to your breath when you have a fright? You take a sharp intake of breath, perhaps to help sustain you through what might be about to happen. It's chesty and fight/flight mode.

What about laughing? Belly laughing? Recall something funny and have a good laugh. How/ where does it feel? How does you feel immediately afterwards?

Tools for Embodying The Real Me

What happens to your breath (and body) when you're sad? Heavy? and almost imperceptible breath? Feel.

What happens to your breath and body when you're angry? Tension, strong long inhale and exhale, or short puffy breaths? Feel.

You're in creative Flow. How is your breath? Feel.

Add in any others I may have missed.

Yes, imagine it and act it out. Did you also feel what happens in your body with these emotions?

Take a few relaxed breaths and come back to yourself.

Your breath and body are very much a mirror of *The Real Me* in the moment, and *The Real Me* is about awareness, so bring your awareness back to your breath as many times a day as you can. Notice breath changes during your day or with any emotional triggers. Ground your feet on the floor as you do your 5 rounds of breath.

It's The Real Me right here, right now. Keep practising.

2. Meditation Practice

"There is no good or bad meditation — there is simply awareness or non-awareness. To begin with, we get distracted a lot. Over time, we get distracted less. Be gentle with your approach, be patient with the mind, and be kind to yourself along the way."
(A Puddicombe, Headspace)

The Real Me

This week, along with grounded breathing, you'll set aside 5 or 10 minutes each day, to establish a meditation practice. You might follow your breathing & grounding practise with your meditation practise. And I want you to commit to this for a whole week. Every day. You may like to work on this twice a day, especially if you already have a regular or intermittent meditation practice.

Meditation? It's like spending quiet, quality time...with yourself!

We'll start with 5 minutes. For people who have never meditated before or those of you who think you can't possibly sit still and do nothing for 5 minutes, then you absolutely need to learn and experience meditation. The wonderful thing about meditation is that it brings you back into body awareness and calms your nervous system (engages the PNS) and settles a busy mind. And you may find yourself in a delicious flow-state.

Meditation is another tool to practise awareness and being with yourself in the *Now*. Remember, You actually get to spend some time with *The Real Me* **as** *The Real Me*! The point of meditation, in this context, is not to experience bliss or nirvana or to completely still your mind. The point is to spend a few minutes every day quietly with your awareness turned inward, spending time with yourself. Read through the general instructions below before you begin:

Either follow your grounded breathing with meditation or find 5 minutes when you won't be disturbed in a quiet place. Early morning and evening, dawn and dusk, are great but anytime is the right time, as long as it suits *You*. You can either sit or lay down. If you're going to lay down, then make sure that you're lying in a manner which gives you a very small amount of discomfort which keeps your awareness on your practice. Think Princess and the Pea. It's very easy to lay down to meditate, and within 5 minutes you're asleep.

Tools for Embodying The Real Me

This will happen because of deep fatigue. Place a damp facewash cloth on your forehead or water bottle on your belly; anything to introduce an awareness that you are relaxing and meditating but nothing that's going to be super irritating or dangerous!

Lying down and meditating is quite special. A real gift to yourself. Remember, it's only 5 minutes.

A more formal practice is seated meditation. Maintaining a seated posture generally allows deep calm and prevents falling asleep. Find yourself a comfortable seat; chair or bulky cushion. Symmetry is important so make sure that *your shoulders are above your hips and your spine is long and straight*. If you're sitting in a chair and chairs tend to have a bit of a lean back, please make sure that you've got some kind of a cushion to bring your spine forward so that it is aligned! Ensure that your legs are relaxed, and your feet are resting comfortably on the floor - if you're sitting in a chair. If you're sitting on a cushion on the floor, even if you are comfortable here, you'll have an awareness of the fact that you're sitting, and if your whole body suddenly completely relaxes, you will fall over! That gentle awareness will keep you seated upright.

On a stool   **Seiza**   **On a chair**

(thanks to thewayofmeditation.com.au for images)

The Real Me

For lying meditation, use a posture similar to that we used for breathing practise with a bulky cushion under your legs and flatter cushion under your head.

When seated or lying, we'll begin our practice by introducing ourselves to parts of our body by tensing and releasing. *This is the focused body relaxation technique.* We're going to start by contracting our muscles and relaxing them. In effect, we're using the body as a conduit into *feeling* the relaxation process of meditation.

Start with your feet, making sure they are relaxed on the floor or relaxed sitting or lying. No dangling feet! Begin with scrunching up your toes, firming your feet and then relaxing. And then do the same by scrunching up your calves, your shins, your knees, almost as if you're trying to stop someone from kicking your leg out from under you, and then relax.

Notice if your face scrunches or shoulders or belly move as you scrunch your toes. Simply noticing and allow isolation and relaxation of these body parts. It's challenging, so notice and have fun with it.

Repeat, tensing and relaxing your knees, your thighs, your buttocks. In each case, take a moment to feel what relaxed *really* feels like before you move to the next body part. It's not a slump or a collapse. Good meditation keeps an energy of awareness concurrent with the delight of relaxation; an energized, focused, relaxed state is a state of flow.

Continue up to your belly. It's very difficult to contract your organs but feel as though you're simply drawing your belly in and release. Repeat with your chest, almost caving in your chest and release. Lift up your shoulders to your ears, then stretch them behind you, and in front of you, then back again, and then release.

Tools for Embodying The Real Me

Tense your arms & release, your hands, then release. Your fingers. Release.

Drop your chin towards your chest, scrunch up your face, clench your jaw. Release.

Gently lift or release your head back to a neutral position.

Begin each meditation session with this focused body relaxation technique. Then set a timer for 5 minutes.

When you're in the meditation process, you are drawing your attention away from the outside world, so be sure to gently close your eyes or lower your gaze.

> *"Meditation practice isn't about trying to throw ourselves away and become something better. It's about befriending who we are already."*
> *(Pema Chödrön)*

For your first 5-minute meditation *(exciting!)* bring awareness to your breath, just as you've learned in grounded breathing; inhale and the exhale. Notice the sounds around you; your breath, sounds in the space, and outside. Notice the sensation of clothes on your skin, hands in your lap or laying gently beside. The parts of your body touching the floor and the parts of your body not touching the floor. Notice and accept (sit or lay without moving) any areas of minor discomfort. At any point during the practice, you can move to relieve more major discomfort, or if you notice tension. When the timer sounds, take a few moments before you gently open or raise your eyes and complete your practice. Well done!

Now it's time to reflect on your experience...

The Real Me

Q: How did I feel before my meditation?
Q: What did I notice during my meditation? Physical sensations? Thoughts?
Q: How do I feel after the practice? Compared with before I started?

For your second or subsequent meditation, choose a point on your body, on which to gently focus. Suggestions below.

After you've relaxed each part of your body and tuned in to your natural breath, take your awareness to:

- The space between your eyebrows; third eye. Settle your awareness here for three breaths.

Then

- That little space, the philtrum, between your nose and your mouth. Many people can feel the breath very gently on that part of your body, can you? Keep your awareness here for three breaths.

Then

- The centre of your chest; heart space. Rest your awareness here for three breaths.

Q: With which of those three points did I feel most connected? If you're not sure, pick one. Take your awareness back to that point. Keep your awareness gently there for the remainder of your 5 minutes. Yes, you will find that there will be some thoughts that come up.

Tools for Embodying The Real Me

Meditation is not about the removal of thoughts. Meditation is about not interacting with them.

We observe thoughts like clouds floating in the sky and then return Awareness to the intial point. Allow your awareness to be gentle concentration on that certain part of the body. It is not a hard, gripping, tension-filled concentration. It is a gentle aligning of your awareness on that part of the body.

Allow it to happen. And when your awareness drifts away, gently bring it back.

During meditation, breath is a natural, easy, subtle kind of breath. Unless you're particularly focused on watching your breath as part of your meditation, you don't notice your breath; allow it to come and go as it pleases. Ultimately, the practice is about inviting a deep relaxing flow into your mind-body experience.

It's this flow state that ultimately connects you back to The Real Me. And you can connect with it at any time. It takes only one Breath.

Enjoy your week and come back to any parts of the process. No judgment if you miss a day or morning but commit to returning to the practise the next morning or evening. When you experience how good it feels, you'll keep coming back to it.

And during this week, keep paying attention, noticing emotions and choices.

Who Am I? *The Real Me.*

Chapter 5

The Real Me: Holy and Wholy and Holey

*"I have a body, but I am not my body.
I have a face, but I am not my face."
(Iyanla Vanzant.)*

How was your week of grounded breathing and meditation practice? I'd love to hear your feedback.

Keep it up. Use the grounded breathing or any breathing practice to bring you back to *The Real Me* when struggling, triggered or just to keep it *Real*. Meditation is a practice for life.

The Real Me is not static or a far distant goal, it's both where you are as well as the higher paths you choose every moment; meditation is getting to know you, with you, by you. :-)

The Real Me

Our Chapter 5 title is inspired by Aretha Frankin singing *Wholy Holy* at the New Temple Missionary Baptist Church in 1972. No, I wasn't fortunate enough to have been there, but Sydney Pollack's documentary is worth a look. Each of us is a Holy representation of incredible intelligence. Each of us is Whole, and our mission is re-discovery of our Wholeness. MeRightNow is Holey; full of gaps and misunderstandings.

Wholy, Holy and Holey brings us back to our physical bodies with new eyes and awareness.

Whatever stage of life we might observe ourselves as 'in', we are in possession of a beautiful body with both positive elements of health and mobility and likely some challenges.

Let's consider our body as a temple (Holy).

There are elements around caring for our mental, emotional and physical bodies of which we might be unaware, negatively habituated or blinkered (Holey).

A healthy body-mind enables us to live as a Whole person (Wholey), The Real Me.

> *"And I said to my body softly, 'I want to be your friend.' It took a long breath and replied, 'I have been waiting my whole life for this."*
> *(Nayyirah Waheed)*

As the ancient and modern philosophers readily teach, you are not your body, anymore than you are your mind or your emotions. Perhaps a way of perceiving The Real Me is that we *inhabit* our bodies; our body is a vehicle to get us around, to experience life, to help us get to know *The Real Me*. Our incredible organic and energetic body is an indispensable interface allowing us to experience Me (every part of the Me with which I identify) as well as all people, objects and phenomena I currently identify as Not Me.

Experiencing is Learning, and I experience so much with my physical body.

Learning is challenging and refining my perceptions.

My perceptions are a meeting and merging of my previous understandings and my current experiences.

Indulge me as we consider how our bodies experience our world and surroundings.

We have five organic senses with sense organs (specifically differentiated cells in our eyes, ears, nose, mouth and skin) with neural pathways connecting to our brain. Our senses are like windows opening outwards inviting stimuli; stimuli trigger receptor cells in our retina (eyes) or receptors in other sense organs. Neurons (nerve cells) are fired and send signals to our brain which sorts and integrates these signals. These actions allow us to perceive the world and connect with our environment. Our brain then analyses the data, checks against previous similar situations and send responses back into our bodies. All this within a second or two. If the response needs to be within a microsecond, our body has nervous reflex arcs which cause us to physically respond super-fast without being encumbered by a lengthy trip to the brain (think hand on hotplate, knee-jerk reaction or your peripheral vision picking up a projectile hurtling towards you).

Bear with me a little longer on body/brain connections; I'm going sciency here.

Our gut (small, large intestines) and heart also contain significant numbers of neurons with strong communication pathways with (not simply 'to' or 'from') our brains. The neuron capacity of our gut has been equated to the brain of a cat (New Scientist 2012; belly brain 500 million neurons compared with cat 300 million (Rothe and Dicky, 2005).

According to Johns Hopkins University and a recent Scientific American (Aug 2020), our 'belly brain' (the enteric nervous system) is not considered to actively make decisions. However, "The system is way too complicated to have evolved only to make sure things *move out* of your colon," says Emeran Mayer, professor at UCLA School of Medicine and author of "The Mind-Gut Connection, How the Hidden Conversation Within Our Bodies Impacts Our Mood, Our Choices, and Our Overall Health."

Scientist have learned that about 90 percent of the fibres in our body's longest nerve, the vagus nerve carries information *from* the gut to the brain rather than the converse. There is evidence that medications such as antidepressants affect our gut and show links to Irritable bowel syndrome (IBS). A study of postmenopausal rats has linked an excess of serotonin from SSUI anti-depressants in the rat's gut to regulation of bone mass and osteoporosis. Interestingly, our whole digestive system is considered medically to be part of our external body, as both ends connect to the outside environment.

Why the segue into our belly brain and emerging research? The current and unfolding research is merely a tiny glimpse into the *holistic connections between each and every cell, tissue and system of our bodies with each other.* Taking care of The Real Me is a

The Real Me: Holy and Wholy and Holey

wake-up call to listen to our bodies; our gut feelings, our aches and pains, our tiredness, our medical conditions and consider these in light of a Whole Me communication from my body and between elements of my body. No body part is an Island. We are not a bag of isolated organs thrown together to be fixed or replaced in isolation when a body part breaks down or plays up.

Your Body demands respect.

Whatever may be happening with your schedule, your mind, your work or family, your body demands respect via the choices you make. When you respect and make friends with your body, it enables *The Real Me* to participate in the activities you choose, expand your definition of love, and tune into the wisdom and experience that only your body possess.

Whilst our minds may wander about, our bodies always live right here, in the present moment.

Tuning in to My Body

This week, inquire using these simple questions a few times each day; on the hour if you like.

- How am I feeling?
- Do I need a break?
- Am I relaxing my shoulders? Neck? Legs? Body part of your choice?
- Check in on my posture. Is my spine straight & relaxed?
- Is my breathing relaxed?
- Is my belly soft and relaxed? Tight and anxious?
- Am I hungry? Thirsty?

The Real Me

- Do I need to move?
- Am I ignoring needs of my body right now? In what way?

_____

_____

Print these and post in places you will notice, or use a check-in ping on your phone. You'll find that some will fall away during the course of the week and others will be a welcome reminder to say Hi to your body. (Hi, how's things, what do you need? Thanks for being part of Me and getting me around today!)

Here's my personal favourite: "I needed to use the bathroom half an hour ago. Why am I still sitting here working? (Yes, because I'm in a Flow...) Thanks, body, Let's get up, stretch, move, smile, have a drink and use the bathroom!"

Explore any responses to the following Q. Remember to look out for emotions, feelings, facial expressions, numbers or percentages, even colours.

Q: How would I define my relationship with my body?
Q: Do I care for my body as a friend?
Q: Where would I place my attitude towards my body on a continuum of:

My body is about how I look--------to--------my body is about doing what I love, health and feeling great?

Q: In my self-care routines, what do I prioritize religiously and what tends to slide?

Use the box below as a guide and rank them.

The Real Me: Holy and Wholy and Holey

Perhaps use a Green highlighter for prioritise, Yellow for 'sometimes I'm great at this…' and Red for 'Yep, this is the first to go when I'm tired, busy or cranky'.

Keep in mind that The Real Me is ruthlessly honest! Some may overlap and as always, add your own.

Sleep hygiene (sleep time and no-device wind-down)
Eating regular, healthy food,
Relaxation time (making sure I have some),
Fun time,
Exercise and movement,
Socializing,
Hydrating,
Creative pursuits and hobbies,
Managing excessive tendencies such as overeating, overindulgence in sex, digital diet, overwork,
Personal hygiene,
Applying restricted boundaries to unhealthy habits such as alcohol, smoking,
Managing my emotions,
Other _____
Other _____

Q: Greens: Which of these takes top spot in my list? Why am I firm with this? Why have I prioritized it and keep prioritizing it? If it's 'easy', why is it easy?
Q: How do I feel in my body when I'm prioritizing this element of my personal care?
Q: Reds: Which of these takes bottom spot in my list? Let go of any judgement; notice with compassionate disinterested interest.

The Real Me

Q: Why do I blow-out here?/ why do *I regularly* blow out here? How can I explore this more deeply? Is there a trigger/family of triggers?

Q: How does my body communicate with me? Consider this one for a few moments.

Q: Do I feel I deserve my own care?

Q: Am I generally happy with my body? If no, screwed up face, or below 50%, which elements of my body? Whose criteria may I be using to judge?

Q: Have I ever been happy with my body? If so, what were my life and priorities like then? Have I drifted from *The Real Me*?

Q: Do I look to others to care about me physically, but sideline my own needs? If yes, how does that feel in my body?

Q: Do I not ask help from others *and* sideline my own needs? If yes, how does that feel in my body?

Q: Do I take care of others physically whilst they observe me not caring for myself?

Q: Does my body, my face, my ageing, my weight take up more than 5% of my mental space? If so, why?

Q: Do I worry what others think of me to the point I significantly adjust personal dress, grooming, posture and care practices to suit others?

Q: Do I use my body to manipulate others? If so, how do I feel about that?

Q: Do I experiment with different forms of self-care? Have some stuck?

Q: Can I form solid self-care routines? Am I able to alter these if external circumstances change; if I'm injured or my gym closes, swimming buddy stops coming along, local fruit and veg shop closes?

Q: Revisit the list from point 2. If I was a caring and compassionate friend recommending the top 3 self-care priorities for *The Real You*, what would they be?

Q: Do I believe that I'm all genetics and have no determination over my body?

Lots of Q here and some big ones. Revisit any which caused you big numbers, physical discomfort or other strong reactions.

Respect your body like your wisest teacher.

Assignment for Chapter 5:

Tune Into and Listen to Your Body

This is also great week to organise a yearly or 6-monthly general check up with your local health professionals. Use these as a baseline to make any adjustments to medications, also look for any indicators which may be in the 'normal' range but decidedly on the low/high side of normal. Check with your doctor & health care professionals for any medical supports you may require.

Now, pay attention to your body in all types of situations. This may be quite challenging if your standard operating procedure has been your Mind telling your Body what to do with no dialogue. Listening is a skill you are honing in this inquiry course, and remember, if it's a skill, you can learn it – but you have to practise.

Listening to your body is like any skill; it can be learned and requires practise.

Internal stimuli

But what am I looking and listening for?

- Pain & where it may be located
- Discomfort; acute or chronic? Regular? Triggers?
- General all over body Ease and focused yet relaxed energy/ flow

- Posture; alertness, slumping. How do I hold my body when sitting? Standing in conversation or making a presentation? Working in a group? Cooking, creating, relaxing?
- Illness; run down, colds or other manifestations
- Information from your gut; hungry? indigestion, butterflies, wind, bloating, soft or hard to the touch? General anxiety? How is my gut feeling right now? Remember the Belly Brain and Tune in.
- Tension and relaxation. Which parts of my body are tense right now? Can I relax them?
- General all-over body feelings; alertness, tiredness, achy, heat, cold, fidgety, flow, calm
- General whole-body emotions, elation, disappointment, shock, panic, excitedness, fear
- Sweating, heart pounding, dry mouth
- Low energy or complete fatigue

Listening is one skill, interpreting is another. We're all much more skilled in observation than interpretation. *Our bodies are always communicating with us whether we are paying attention or not.* And if you're super-sensitive, you may want your body to shush so you can get on with Stuff! But more often, in Western and some Eastern societies, I feel, we allow our minds to override unsolicited physical signals if our mind has other ideas about what's important right now, deadlines, 'pressing' issues, emergencies or social/peer pressures.

How do we learn to interpret our body communications? We inquire. Chances are, you might already know some answers but be prepared to not necessarily understand straight away. Uncovering and getting to know *The Real Me* takes time, patience and compassionate attention and our bodies are an amazing lens.

The Real Me: Holy and Wholy and Holey

Q: Why am I sweating right now?
Q: What is my body telling me? (Ask the question, maybe 'Hi, amazing body, what's up?'Listen.)
Q: What's my best and most compassionate response to _____ (whatever I interpret I'm feeling) right now?
Q: How can I honour what my body is telling me?
Q: How can I show honour to my body whilst taking care of business/doing what I love to do?

Your body is a friend not foe, certainly not a weak vessel which needs to be conquered or subdued, forced or press-ganged. Athletes are great at training their body at limits beyond what you or I may attempt whilst still caring for their physical instrument with utmost sensitivity. Honouring and caring for your body not only brings release to some chunky bits that are not *The Real Me* but also ensures you are more Productive and Present and Real when doing activities you care about.

I recall a coarse joke from my childhood which holds more wisdom than the simple blue-collar punchline, which I'll omit. Here's my version:

The organs of the body were having a meeting, trying to decide who was in charge. Each organ took a turn to speak up:

Brain......... I should be in charge because I run all body functions; obviously! Top down management!

Blood......... I should be in charge because I circulate oxygen and nutrients and feed you, brain! And every one of you.

Stomach......... I should be in charge because I process food to you, brain! And all of you. Want to starve?

The Real Me

Legs......... I should be in charge because I take the lot of you where you want to go. Wanna be a tree? No!

Eyes......... I should be in charge because I see to gather food and supplies and keep you all from harm.

Rectum......... I should be in charge because I get rid of your waste.

At the rectum's response, the other body parts laughed so hard that the rectum was insulted. To prove their point, the rectum immediately slammed tightly closed and stayed that way for 6 days, refusing to rid the body of any waste whatsoever.

Day 1 – Brain got a terrible headache and cried out for relief
Day 2 – Stomach got bloated and began to ache terribly
Day 3 – Legs got cramps and became unstable
Day 4 – Eyes became watery, and vision became blurred
Day 5 – Blood became toxic and poisoned the body
Day 6 – The other organs agreed to let the rectum (asshole) be in charge.

Okay, so I included the punchline.

With no weight given to the dubious social commentary, when we allow our whole mind/body to flow and operate in synchronicity, we are a magnificent instrument for good with endless possibilities; *The Real Me*.

External stimuli

Now practise using your physiological radar regarding your external environment. Which perceived external situations trigger your body?

The Real Me: Holy and Wholy and Holey

Q: In certain situations, do I notice butterflies? A knot in my stomach? Tension? Which situations?

Q: In certain situations, do I notice heart pounding, tight chest, dry or constricted throat? Tears? What environments stimulate these feelings?

Q: Do particular environments feel calming? Open? Claustrophobic? Terrifying?

Q: When I'm with certain people do I feel tingly? Relaxed? With others does my skin crawl or do I notice heightened awareness of some kind?

Q: Do I vote with my feet (as I find myself walking away? Towards?) in some situations? What kinds of situations?

Q: Do certain physical spaces, nature, certain people seem to bring out *The Real Me*; relaxed and fully aware? In Flow?

Is it possible to mis-interpret body signals? Yes and yes. Some of the most common misinterpretations are related to sugar, caffeine and fatigue. If you slump mid-afternoon and reach for processed sugar or a caffeine hit, consider that you've trained your body through habitual white-drugging to be looking for these hits. White drugging is my term for culturally acceptable uppers. Google *'is sugar a drug'* for some interesting reading.

If I hit a mid-afternoon slump, I ask myself the question – do I need a rest or do I need a walk? On days I feel too exhausted to even respond, I know it's nanna-nap time. If I need a walk, I know it and often find myself heading towards my walking shoes before my brain has even caught up with the question (ie voting with my feet). I accept it's time to put down my work for now.

Consider that some of your personal interpretations of body signals may be misinterpretations and pay attention. Keep inquiring and listening.

The Real Me

"When the internal signals you receive from your body match your values and the actions you take, you will likely feel calm, peaceful and aligned. When you are not aligned (in other words, when you override your body's signals and take action that is different from what you really want) you may feel overwhelmed, upset or disconnected."
(Ilona de Ruijter)

This week, continue to work with your grounding breath practise and daily mediation. Keep noticing and pay particular attention to your body. Your body is always in the present moment. Use your awareness of your body and One Breath to return to *The Real Me* at any moment. Breath and body, always in the present. Centre, and bring yourself back to the here and now.

Give loving thanks to your body for its part in your amazing life, adventures and experiences. The Real Me *dwells here.*

"Your body is your vehicle for life.
As long as you are here, live in it.
Love, honor, respect and cherish it,
treat it well, and it will serve you in kind."
(Suzy Prudden)

Chapter 6

Creating The Real Me

This week we're halfway through the course!

Creation or Stagnation? It's your choice. There's no middle option.

Take a moment to breathe, feel your body and celebrate your re-connection with yourself. We tend to fixate on the mountain in front of us and forget to look behind at the mountains, swamps, deserts and frozen wastes we've already traversed. How are you feeling? What's different in yourself and your life?

Q: What's *realer* in your life right now?

Three things:
I'm _____
I've noticed _____
I'm exploring _____

The Real Me

Keep up your breathing and meditation practices. A handful of minutes each day will bring you back to You. What's next? Creativity.

> *"Creativity means to push open the heavy, groaning doorway to life."*
> *(Daisaku Ikeda)*

So far, we've investigated uncovering, discovering and recovering *The Real Me*, so creating *The Real Me?* might come as a bit of a surprise. We're not creating *The Real Me* from scratch or building something that is not already there. *The Real Me* IS here all the time, and we are learning to recognise, value and release *Me* out into the world and re-discovering Me in our own inner worlds. We're chipping away bits of our outer casing to uncover (expose!) and live our *Realness*; like tapping a piece of limestone casing to uncover an opal.

The reason this chapter is called *Creating The Real Me* simply because it's about creativity. Creativity is something that you might view as something nice to do, maybe in a bit of spare time or you might see yourself as not being creative at all. Conversely, you may already recognise Creativity as a foundational element of *The Real Me*.

Take a look around you. The chair you're sitting on at home, or the seat on the bus, train or Uber was not only dreamed up and designed by somebody being creative, it was actually built physically by them or others. Every single manufactured item you see around you is creativity or copy. We are surrounded by, clothed in, protected by the creativity of others.

Take a moment to look around *now* with intention to notice.

Creating The Real Me

Your home, your book, your phone, the room you are in and its elements, the clothes you are wearing; all of these things were dreamed up and created by someone, or by many people. Nature has a way of creating itself and you likely have your own ideology here, but a great many of the physical, visual and musical items or programmes in your experience are indeed creations; products of people's imaginations, refined, planned and executed, to be brought forth into something that you can hold, hear, see, feel, touch, and enjoy.

Consider creativity not as something which is an add-on or an attribute that isn't really you, but as something that is essential both to your life, and also to who you *Really* are. It's absolutely essential.

"Oh no, I'm not a creative person!" you might say.

My husband says this often, meanwhile creating beautifully serene images and inspiring messages for our Yoga posts. In the West, it's been part of our culture to ignore, suppress, ridicule and denigrate our (and others) creativity. We also have many stereotypes of struggling artists. Consider the Deep Truth that we are ALL creative and that creativity can be defined and re-defined in many different ways. As many as there are people on Earth. Creativity is both a continuum and evolving aspect of our lives.

During the Covid-19 pandemic, The Arts was one of the first areas of daily life to be shut down; it was considered by governments to be non-essential! In this chapter, we're bringing our Real Me to life, exploring our creativity in whichever areas we choose. We create; we flow. That's our assignment for this week.

The Real Me creates; it's as simple as that.

The Real Me

Let's explore different areas of creativity; I'm going to challenge you and you're going to challenge yourself.

This week's challenge is to notice creativity all around you *and* be creative in areas of your life in which you feel most comfortable, most joyful, and most light. You may already know your creative leanings so start here. If not, peruse the list below and notice what jumps out at you.

> *"Creativity is the sudden cessation of stupidity."*
> *(Edwin Land)*

Using the list below, highlight your top three; the three elements of creativity that resonate most with you, the ones that you tend to lean most towards, the ones which light you up simply thinking about them. And you might be surprised at some inclusions and think, 'well that's not creative, that's just what I do,' but there's a real element of creativity in all of these pursuits. I've included spaces for other ideas that might come to you intuitively. So, grab your highlighter, and have a browse!

- **Music:** playing, listening, teaching, recording, and choosing music for others.
- **Decorating:** cakes, houses, rooms, bench tops, work-spaces, floral arranging, scrap-booking, and decorating with colour.
- **Fashion:** how you dress, clothes in which you dress others, dressmaking, and design.
- **Gardening:** landscaping, potting and growing, and re-decorating outside living spaces.
- **Writing:** screenwriting, stories, poetry, journaling, song writing, editing and blogging.

- Cooking: creating meals & recipes, cheffing, plating, baking and edible art.
- Traditional forms of art: painting, drawing, colouring, scrapbooking and sculpture.
- Digital and virtual art: making movies, clips and creating games.
- Creating social events: myriads of ways to bring people together.
- Creative photography: film, digital, and videography.
- Speaking: motivational, encouraging, and marketing. Making conversation. Speaking my truth.
- Traditional crafts: knitting, sewing, crochet, card-making, jewellery making, and pottery.
- Movement: dance, Yoga, skipping, roller-skating, gym routines, skydiving, martial artistry, and physical arts.
- Hair and beauty: hairdressing, manscaping, poodle trimming, manicuring and makeup.
- Creating safe spaces, opportunities, meaningful tasks and jobs for others.
- Creating learning experiences for others to connect and thrive.
- Building: architecture, functional spaces, sandcastle-making, and fencing.
- Others _____
- Others _____

You may hone in on some of these elements that you regularly use for work. Your creativity is a part of any work you do; consider. This week, however, choose between two and five creative elements from the list above and we're going to put them into action.

When you have your top two (possibly more), let's rank them. Say for example, your first two were music and gardening, ask yourself:

The Real Me

"If I had to choose one or the other of those two, if I could only do one and I could never do the other one, which one would I rank as most important to me?"

Ask the question, let the answer come up from where these beautiful answers come from; *The Real Me*. This is an exercise in ranking and invoking your *Real Me*; it doesn't mean to say that you can never garden if you put gardening second. Use this method to rank your top two then your top five, in some kind of order. Allow your list to sit for a moment.

Q: To what creative ideas am I really drawn?
Q: How does it make me feel to simply contemplate creativity + me right now?
Q: Was there a creative category which lit me up for a moment before I discarded? Oh, I could never... Explore.
Q: Did I choose safe? Scary?

Yes, I put skydiving and roller-skating in the list for a reason!

Or are you surprised how much you'd like to groom poodles or write a play? If unusual creative pursuits come up for you, it's part of *The Real Me*. No doubt. If you explore, you'll know where it comes from and perhaps why you have left it on the shelf for many years. Breathe. Smile. This is wonderful, excavating & revealing work.

Here are some other ideas about creativity for you to consider:

1. First and foremost, *creativity feeds The Real Me*. Creativity both nourishes and expresses the most authentic elements of yourself. You might go so far as to say creativity IS *The Real Me,* so finding and allowing ways to express your creativity daily is a way of expressing the real you in

different situations of everyday life. Simply noticing your moments and periods of expression and creativity within work and everyday life is nourishing.

2. Secondly, your flowstate is most likely to arise within your creative endeavours; *the attention you pay during the creative process **is** your flow*, and not necessarily the outcome or finished product. This process of creating and flow is releasing, nurturing, balancing and deeply healing.

3. Next, notice *language* around creativity. As mentioned, my husband has said, *"Oh, I'm not a creative person!"* and many of us remember our paintings at school and cast doubt on our ability to create. And yet I would observe him spending an hour putting together a beautiful image, choosing fonts, images and words; playing with colour and moving things around and I'd say to him, *"You know, that's incredibly creative!"*

Q: Who set my definition of creativity? Can I re-define creativity in a way that is specific to me?

Q: Can I use the word 'creative' about tasks that I'd previously considered routine?

4. Here it comes. When it comes to creativity, our minds and societal training barge in and say learned things like:

   "Frivolous! What use is there in music/art/that incredible new color on your wall? You can't make a living doing that! Do something useful with your time! Well, that's all very well but you could have been washing the car, cleaning the house - what about all those jobs that need doing?"

Any of these sound familiar? If someone else isn't saying it, are you saying it to yourself; an echo of childhood training? We are aware that our mind will make judgments about what's creative and what's not. And we're also aware that the mind is NOT creative; it's an impossibility. Our mechanical minds can be taught and skilled in many aspects that we use as allies of our creativity – chord playing and finger shifting when playing guitar, painter's brushwork, ideal consistency of our potters' clay - but the creativity itself comes from *The Real Me* and not our mind. If we've absorbed large chunks of *judgmental* during our lives, we can still be practicing awareness and unlearning in this aspect of our recovery.

Each of us must lovingly accept and explore our inner creative spirit and nurture it. Full stop!

So, notice the language that you use yourself around creativity. Are you judging the outcome as no good rather than enjoying the flow, challenge and joy of creating? Again, notice and release any judgment; notice the creative language you use or *hear in your head* every day for the rest of this week.

Assignment for Chapter 6

Let's Create

Each day for the next seven days, set aside somewhere between 10 and 30 minutes each day; *yes, each day,* & perhaps an hour or two over the weekend or a non-work day. Prioritize this as if you were going to write an essay on it for grading or a work task with a deadline. Pick something from your list and start acting on it. You might decide not to begin with your first choice as it may not be the ideal time to garden, or you need more than 10 minutes to get out your paints and canvases.

Listen to the *Inner Me*. You may chop and change with pure excitement or perhaps, once you start at the top of your list, there may be no going back, and you might stick with your creative outlet for the whole week - or longer! As always, it's completely your choice. Don't worry if it feels a little forced or weird or crazy at first.

Whilst creating, does it *feel* creative? Pulling out and tuning up your old guitar? Playing or creating that playlist that you've been meaning to do for a long time? Dancing around the living room with the kids/cat/dog? Putting together a different outfit, for either yourself or one of your kids for the next day? Going outside and putting those plants in the garden or repotting for the balcony? Anything on your list and more. Feel into your experience.

10 to 30 minutes each day. Yes, some days you will be hard pressed to allocate time; perhaps in the evening, to sit down and making a sketch of something. Even 5 minutes; find a pencil, charcoal; a ballpoint pen and sketch something on the back of an envelope!

The experience is to really immerse yourself into yourself as yourself, immersed in your creative experience, doing something that really feels creative to you, for you and by YOU. Notice if and when you feel in flow (even microseconds) and how you feel during that time, notice emotions and body sensations.

Do you feel Open? Light? Grounded? Focused? Relaxed? Notice any emotions that came up in this space. Frustration? Interruption? Judgement? Any heaviness and ugly thoughts coming up for you, such as:

'I'm no good at this? Why bother? It's lousy. It's not perfect?'

Who's judging? Certainly not The Real Me, (*The Real Me* is having a ball). Notice and let go. Remember, creativity is about the process, not necessarily loving the outcome every time. It's a learning process

The Real Me

of 'I can create' and also giving yourself permission to explore and discover *The Real Me* via the process of creation.

> *"Creativity is allowing yourself to make mistakes. Art is knowing which ones to keep."*
> *(Scott Adams)*

Over the weekend or on a day that you're not working, take 1 to 2 hours and either tackle something a little larger, or give yourself the time and space for real immersion. This can be solitary or co-creational; with others. Keep in mind whilst you're exploring *The Real Me* within the context of being creative, the apparently collaborative space of creating with, or alongside others, will throw other issues into the mix. For example, if you're painting with your children, especially little ones, their needs will always be paramount. If you're making a music video with friends or planning a garden space with a partner, creative differences and variances in your communication styles may become apparent. The experience may be connecting & rewarding and may be more (or less) personally nourishing than you anticipate.

Planning time might be part of that couple of hours. If you've come up with or discovered an inspirational recipe, this might simply be time that you take creatively to shop and plan. If you're moved to create an event for others to get together, it might be the time you take to connect with other people and book a place to meet up. If you're writing, drawing, or painting, you may start working on an idea that's been knocking at your creative door for a little while.

Sit - or stand or move - and create! Work from a stream of consciousness flow; always with no expectation. If you're inspired by flowers, you may want to arrange a small or a huge bunch of flowers, perhaps for a friend, or even for yourself; choose the flowers and come home and do the arranging. Immerse yourself into something that you've tuned into being creative for you.

> *"The chief enemy of creativity is good sense."*
> *(Pablo Picasso)*

Honestly, this is the part of the course that some people are likely to skip out on. It just seems like if there's anything that you *think* doesn't really necessarily bring out *The Real Me*, this might be it. You might see the creativity as that bit of extra fluff around the edges of life that you just don't have time for. But creativity is so much more than that. We are created. We are creative. The whole of our *Being* **is** being creative.

Flow and Creativity: In the Everyday

The little things you do every day; the things that you might see as being mundane and trivial, many of them are – or could be – creative acts. Think about when you *make* yourself or others a cup of coffee or tea. The attention that you put into this small act of creation; making something special, either just how you like it or something a bit different; that's creativity. When you wipe down a bench the dancing of your hand and cloth, creativity; when you get out the gloves, spade or chainsaw and do a bit of work in the garden, creativity; your self-care routines in the morning, cleaning and drying your body, the way you apply deodorants and oils; it's all creativity.

Notice the simple creative elements inherent in these everyday tasks, when we are really paying attention to the sensations and patterns in each moment of being *The Real Me*. Allow, notice, expand.

The Real Me

Often, it's the language that we use. We think things are jobs, we are taught that they are chores. We've been raised to label them as such. Maybe, if we find a little bit of creativity in each and everything that we do, we find that we're creating all the time. It's a buzz and it's what we're here to do. We're here to create & discover ourselves through our creations. Our life is indeed our creation. The things that we make, the joy that we bring to others, each of these acts of creation continually feed back into creating ourselves.

> *"Creativity is the natural order of life. The refusal to be creative is self-will and is counter to our true nature."*
> *(Julia Cameron)*

Here are our inquiry questions for this week:

Q: How did I feel about creativity (or MY creativity) at the start of this week? End of this week?
Q: In which way/s did I express my creativity today?
Q: Why did I express my creativity in this way? (This might be your list activity, where you might also come up with extra things you can label as creative)!
Q: Did I enjoy creating?
Q: What issues or judgments came up during this process?
Q: Are there any old beliefs, language, thoughts or emotions around creativity I've been able to challenge and release?
Q: How did it make me feel?
Q: Did I feel in flow at any time during my creative pursuits?
Q: Did I inspire others to create, or did I notice any other flow-on effects of my choices?

Did you notice feelings of lightness, space, peace, joy and even the mood you might be in when you're midway through your dedicated creative time? Did you feel engaged, focused and relaxed – maybe even in flow state?

If you're at the point where you're really stuck choosing areas in which you might be creative, consider some of the pursuits that you enjoyed in childhood. Back in those days, when there was much less pressure in terms of taking care of families, looking after others, information overload, pressures of work and of course, finances - all the things that us grown-ups deal with on a daily basis. In life when days were long, and life was perhaps a little simpler. Think back to the things that you liked doing. When the days stretched on forever, what would you actually choose to do?

> *"You do not need anybody's permission to live a creative life."*
> *(Elizabeth Gilbert)*

Well, actually you do. *You need your own permission.* Open, allow, and create.

Further Reading:

"The Artist's Way" by Julia Cameron.

Cameron will lead you to explore creativity in detail in the context of your own life, and some of the ideas in Chapter 6 are drawn from Cameron's work. Recommended!

The Real Me

Chapter 7

Tapping Into the Superpowers of *The Real Me*

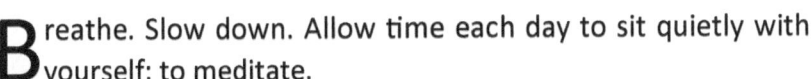

Breathe. Slow down. Allow time each day to sit quietly with yourself; to meditate.

Allow & prioritise space in your schedule to continue with your creative pursuits this week.

Week 7 is big. It allows you to explore a different Superpower each day and each one offers an exercise with which you can engage.

Each of these Superpowers is a nourishing & transformative quality of *The Real Me*. Take as long as you need to explore each one and practise within your day or allow some to expand into a few days. As you feel and as you wish, proceed. Come back to those with which you connect most strongly, feel most nourishing - or are most challenging.

> *"We can only be said to be alive in those moments when our hearts are conscious of our treasures."*
> *(Thornton Wilder)*

This week we will expand our awareness and reclaiming of *The Real Me* by bringing greater or more focused attention to particular aspects of each moment which can nourish us deeply. We'll explore our relationships with the following Superpowers:

Beauty, Gratitude, Play, Curiosity, Compassion and Courage

Each of these Cheerleaders bring us into regular moments of *The Real Me* and help us to see, create & live *The Real Me* with clarity.

Beauty: Beauty Mirrors The Soul

Let's begin this week with a Beautiful day.

Beauty. What does the word beauty conjure up for you?

There is an admirer of beauty within all of us. Beauty is in the eye of the beholder - it's an overused & somewhat tired cliché; however, explore the idea that we all recognise beauty in some form when we behold it. Beauty might take our breath away, still our chattering mind for a long inhale as we take it all in, a WOW moment of transcendence. It can almost feel like a connection to something greater than ourselves. Perhaps it is.

Tapping Into the Superpowers of The Real Me

Imagine yourself in the presence of something you find beautiful; a sunrise, a sunset, a forest or mountain scene, a piece of art or jewellery, the face or voice of a person loved; symmetry or asymmetry, the smell of a favourite meal cooking, the touch of silk, a beloved piece of music, favourite shape or colour, or a warm bubble bath. Beauty can be found in so many moments and details whether they are natural to Mother Earth or created by ourselves or fellow humans.

We can purchase beauty when we buy a new item, something desired and planned for weeks, then enjoy it for months or years. We can witness the flow of a meaningful sentence onto a page; the evening sunlight on thousands of leaves. I particularly love those moments of sheer beauty when children are happy and dancing around the house or playing in the garden. And the motivation to buy or gift a new plant – simple beauty. I love seeing someone leaving our local market, garden shop or a friend's house with a plant; nursing both the moment of beauty and life but also supporting an ultimate goal – to bring more beauty into their homes and gardens; into their everyday lives.

> *"The object of education is to*
> *teach us to love what is beautiful."*
> *(Plato, The Republic)*

Universal beauty is experienced when observing sunsets, views from hilltops and mountain tops, songs and music that touch us deeply, whispers of cool air on hot skin, even a cup of our favorite brew. We often engage our five senses when observing beauty: the soothing smells of flowers, invigorating smells of coffee or lemons. Do you know anyone who doesn't love the newborn baby smell or freshly cut grass? These are all essences of beauty.

The Real Me

I'm noticing a circular pattern of light on my ordinary metal water bottle that sits in front of me. Mystifying beauty which draws me into a moment of simple awareness. I become aware of lightness and stillness and become part of the beauty itself. Large or small moments of beauty capture us and hold us spellbound in that moment, then return us to the present with delight. *If we notice them.* If more and more moments in my life become delightful, how can I not be living a delightful life?

Do you notice that in all of the examples, the beauty is a fleeting and momentary quality? Any beauty we experience is always in the present moment, before something else captures our attention, or our mind greys and wanders away. Even to realise we're in the presence of beauty, we must be paying attention.

Can we expand our personal definition of beauty? In the 2011 sci-fi movie *"Another Earth"*, a troubled young woman wins an essay competition to travel to another Earth. She describes an astronaut's story in which he was bothered by an interminable *"drip, drip, drip"* sound on a solo return from a mission. He spends hours, then sleepless days fruitlessly searching for the source of the sound, then trying to block it out. At the point of insanity, he experienced a moment of clarity. He listened and tuned in to every drip, very intently. She reports that he was able to fall in love with the sound and spent the remaining space days in absolute bliss.

I love that story and can report personal success with a ticking clock and a barking dog, though not so much with a front-end loader, working for hours in the easement next to my house.

Our relationship with beauty is a deeply personal one and this makes recognizing and experiencing Beauty without attachment an important part of restoring *The Real Me*. Physical beauty of any kinds is always fleeting; moments, days, years or millennia; any physical item from flowers to our bodies to stars will eventually decay. Hoarding beauty turns it to clutter, grasping at beauty can cause real harm to ourselves and others and cause your *Real Me* to be stuck and buried by stuff or harmful behaviours. Consider the following:

What I find beautiful is actually a reflection of The Real Me and is not external at all.

Beauty Inquiry Questions:
What Is My Relationship With Beauty?

Q: What objects, experiences or moments do I find engagingly beautiful? List a few.
Q: Can I experience flow, mental pause and the beauty of *The Real Me* in those moments?
Q: Do I actively seek beauty in my life?
Q: How do I purposely engage with beauty, daily, weekly, monthly, yearly?
Q: How does being in the presence of beauty make me feel? (Experience is understanding).
Q: Am I able to expand my concept of beauty to notice beauty in the ordinary?
Q: Every minute or so, can I take a moment to notice something beautiful – or the beauty in something ordinary?
Q: Do I like to create beauty? In which forms? Do I share this beauty with others?
Q: Am I able to accept others' definitions of beauty; those which are not my own?
Q: Can I interrogate my physical surroundings for elements of beauty? (Sometimes we remain unaware of beauty until it startles

us from our work, or a mindless activity, or from our personal greying-out-miles-away moment).

Q: Can I notice the Beauty of simply being *The Real Me* in the imperfect present moment *Right Now*? (Even with an itchy foot, sore back or feeling a little hot or cold, or hearing the noisy chainsaw next door)?

Q: Does the experience of beauty ever trigger feelings of inadequacy, sadness, when I mentally rebound the experience into judging myself via criteria of others?

Q: Am I able to recognise and centre myself within the beauty of The Real Me? How does it feel?

> *"Beauty is happiness. It's the images and moments that inspire and represent the most distinct and remarkable attractiveness of our souls. It's the moment we feel free and real. It's the moments we feel proud and eminent. It's the moments we feel alive."*
> *(Lexi Herrick)*

Inner beauty shines out. It's *The Real Me* inside and out. Apply, learn, unlearn, re-learn and explore beauty in many moments, today and each day. Take a few moments to reflect on the Beauty you've experienced today and your personal experience of a Beautiful Day.

Exercise: The last Inquiry Question circles back to our meditation practise. Perhaps you'd like to meditate on beauty during your Beauty practise today.

Tapping Into the Superpowers of The Real Me

Gratitude: The Gift You Give Yourself

*"**Gratitude** is not only the greatest of virtues, but the parent of all others."*
(Cicero)

Day 2 of this week is a *Greatful*, grateful Day.

Gratitude, grateful, gratefulness. Grace. Gratitude is defined as quality of being thankful; a *"readiness to show appreciation for and to return kindness"* (Oxford). Cambridge qualifies with *"strong appreciation"* and I'll qualify further with *genuine appreciation*. All the qualities of *The Real Me* that we're refuelling and re-discovering are based on our reconnecting with our genuineness and authenticity; our true nature.

Gratitude is a Superpower and a defining quality of *The Real Me*, though the very few English words we use to describe and express gratitude fall short of the strength, depth and breadth of feelings we can experience when being grateful or thankful. It's an acknowledgement of our connection with, and appreciation for, others.

"Thank you, Thanks! Many thanks, I really appreciate it! I'm very grateful for this! Thank you so much! My gratitude abounds. Yes, Yes, Yes!"

That's about the extent of verbal gestures of gratitude in the English lexicon. Thankfully, our gratitude can also be expressed non-verbally – a wave in traffic, a gesture, hug, gift or a huge smile – imagine a child finally receiving a doll, special outfit or game console they've been waiting for all year.

The Real Me

I once heard local radio show hosts discussing the social norms of a return wave when a driver pulls over for you. You might wave to say 'thanks', and sometimes they wave back. Would I experience feeling dissed or put-out if a driver – who was the courteous party, after all – didn't return my wave? No; I'm happy that they've done me a service. One of the radio hosts was most put out if the generous driver didn't acknowledge the acknowledgment! People are funny. Gratitude itself is simple stuff but an incredibly powerful way of expressing *The Real Me* in a way that both nourishes ourselves — the giver — as well as the receiver. But are we grateful enough? Too much? Somewhere within the continuum is The Real Me. How do others interpret our gratitude and how does this impact our lives and relationships? Let's explore.

The Real Me expresses simple gratitude when another person has kindly undertaken a task for us; given a few moments of their life to help us out *and we have both noticed and acknowledged*. It's simple, direct connection between you and another. *I* Thank *You*. In the case of 'paying it forward' the kindness may be random and we may never receive actual thanks from the person who benefited.

An fMRI study asked participants to imagine they were Holocaust survivors who had received gifts such as shelter or lifesaving food from strangers, and found that people who indicated and imagined that they would feel more grateful in these scenarios had more brain activity in the brain regions associated with moral cognition, perspective shaping, and *reward*. (Fox, G et al, 2015)

Gratitude engages the reward centres of **our own brains**.

Consider this for a moment. The Boomerang effect of thanking someone, a group or ourselves, rebounds more positive feeling to ourselves. *We* feel rewarded having offered gratitude.

Tapping Into the Superpowers of The Real Me

Neuroscientist Christina Karn's 2018 research supports that more grateful people also have stronger neural pathways of altruism (selfless concern for the wellbeing of others) and that people expressing more gratitude appeared to have more altruistic brains, as shown by the response of their brain areas associated with feelings of reward.

Karn cites that, "Not only does gratitude go along with more optimism, less anxiety and depression, and greater goal attainment, but it's also associated with fewer symptoms of illness and other physical benefits." Sounds like *The Real Me*!

Are we strengthening this neural pathway by practising gratefulness? Karn et al concluded Yes, this neural response *can* be strengthened: it was stronger in participants who had been assigned to keep a gratitude journal for three weeks, than it was in participants who were assigned a different (non-gratitude) journaling activity. This suggests that practicing gratitude changes the brain in a way that orients people to feel more rewarded when other people benefit, which could help explain why gratitude positively affects relationships. More on this in Chapter 10.

Many of us expand our experience of gratitude to include a divine quality. For example, when we have beautiful weather for a sports carnival or holiday, finding a car park in a crowded place, family members return home safe after a day's activity, saying Grace at meals, or considering any of the incredible blessings we experience in daily life. 'Thank God' is a common cultural release, whether or not we are intentionally offering thanks to a deity.

Gratitude has another dimension in hindsight, during difficulty when a moment or event did not run to your ideal or mental plan and you've experienced emotions ranging from, *'that's interesting'* to downright annoyed, or further intensified to a difficult situation of authentic and deep grief. Whilst you may shrink from being grateful in this type of situation, you may at some point, perhaps months or years later, be grateful for deeper understandings you have gained through this experience. You may find new and satisfying connections or deeper relationships formed in the aftermath, compassion and the opportunity to learn and discover more about *The Real Me* through these unsolicited challenges. Sit for a moment, eyes closed or lowered and ask the question:

Q: What is something I feel grateful about, *Right Now*? And no judgement if it's the coffee and cake sitting in front of me, a compliment paid to me, the sun warming my back, family or children, my measure of health, being alive, a special gift recently received or a message from a friend. Or the good fortune of a friend or community personally known or unknown to us. Or all of the above.

Studies in gratitude have burgeoned since the year 2000 in areas of neuroscience, medicine, ecology and sociology, as well as psychology. Gratitude has been linked to cognitive thinking areas of our brain, as well as emotional brain centers. Our culture, disposition, personality traits, moods and genetics – and gender, also affect both our experience, and expression of gratitude. Interestingly, men (US study, Kashdan etal 2009) showed less gratitude than women and US males, less than German males. And there is a gene linked to gratitude! Unsurprisingly, lack of sleep affects your likelihood of expressing gratitude. (When are we ever *The Real Me* when sleep deprived?)

Gratitude questions, these don't come easy. Consider some of these now and take the awareness with you into your Grateful day.

Gratitude Inquiry Questions:
What's My Relationship With Gratitude?

Q: How do I feel when I am genuinely grateful to someone? (Notice beyond identification with *"I feel grateful"*. Notice accompanying emotion – surprise, relief, happiness... as well as feeling – joy, peace, and love. How does it feel in my body? What is my breath response? Experiencing openness, a sense of lifting and lightness? Or is there some apprehension; fear of being expected to provide something in return? Each situation may be different.

Q: How does this feeling of gratitude change when the person is in front of me? When I'm thanking them in an email? In my imagination? When I'm expressing gratitude for having fresh food and water, gratitude to a divine being, the universe or having just avoided an accident?

Q: Do I ever express gratitude when it's not genuine? Why? How does this feel?

Q: How many times a day do I express gratitude? By all means, keep a tally today; otherwise simply notice – every time. Observe and analyze. No judgement.

Q: Notice gratitude around you. Who's displaying it? Who rarely displays gratefulness?

Q: Does expressing gratitude ever leave me feeling weak? Cold? Afraid? (any emotional response to the exercise above?) Explore.

Q: How does it feel for me when others express gratitude to me? How do I receive this, emotionally? Feelings? In my body? Breath? What do I say? Does it depend on any other factors (hangry? Sleep deprived? Stressed or distracted?)

Q: Does my reception of gratitude from another depend on how I perceive the person - do I like or trust them - or their motivation? Does it depend on any other factors (hangry? Sleep deprived? Stressed or distracted?)

Q: Do I feel comfortable asking for help??? Receiving help if offered?

Q: How do I respond to perceived ingratitude from others? Do I expect a certain response when helping others? How do I respond – physically, emotionally, in breath – when this doesn't play out?
Q: Are there certain people or groups I refuse to assist due to perceived lack of gratitude?
Q: Does lack of gratitude from others chip at my own self esteem?
Q: Do some people refuse to show warmth and gratitude as a control mechanism over me to keep me trying to please them?
Q: Do I over-thank others and display a Mr. or Ms. super-nice personality in order to control others? Is this authentic?
Q: Are my gratitude responses free flowing in the moment? Automated? Carefully considered before I allow one to 'escape'?
Q: What is the Gratitude barometer like in my household, if family members are living with me? Is gratitude a 'thing' my family does? My culture does?

Jones and Wong (2017) showed that a 3 week gratitude intervention (journaling and letter writing) demonstrated greater activation in the medial prefrontal cortex (attention and motivation) area of the brains of the participants, plus improved mental health at the end of the three weeks. These changes persisted when re-tested 3 months after the intervention. Gratitude re-aligns your brain, mind and awareness with *The Real Me*. It's a Superpower, use it wisely and often.

Apply, learn, unlearn, re-learn and explore gratitude in many moments, today and each day. Reflect on your Grateful Day.

Exercise: Circle back to our meditation practise. Perhaps you'd like to meditate on gratitude during your practice today. Some people report that a gratitude meditation is their favourite. You may have a particular person/event on whom to meditate, or simply use the words 'Thank you.' My favourite is 'Thank you for the love in my life.' And I use it every day. Trial it yourself.

Tapping Into the Superpowers of The Real Me

Play and Fun: There's No Me Without Play

"All work and no play makes Jack a dull boy."
(Proverb)

No, not child's play; adult play, our play, we play, I play. Today is Play Day.

Do I Play?

Playing is engaging in activity for enjoyment and recreation, rather than a serious or practical purpose. Play used to have image issues. We may have played happily as children but at a particular stage of life we absorbed the message that 'you're not a child anymore. You need to work, not play.' Historically, play has been viewed as a frivolous use of our time, particularly when we're working hard to make ends meet. In the old days, a lady or gentleman of leisure benefited from independent means and could play all day, whereas the rest of us worked to support our families. Some cultures and working classes thus have a historical suspicion of play. Today, being a Gamer is a thing and we're reconnecting with play on a larger scale. What do *I* think of play?

"The opposite of play is not work; it's depression."
(Dr. Stuart Brown)

Dr. Brown's clinical research supports this statement. *We all need time to play* and allow the play to be fun, possibly unstructured, even if just for a few minutes a day. Yes, there are always things to do, always and forever Ameen and Amen. Are we able to set pressing but not urgent matters aside to play? To have fun? For many of us, this is a real struggle until we understand and experience the necessity of play. Play, fun and lightness of spirit is an important

The Real Me

part of discovery and recovery of *The Real Me*. The time we spend playing is on a continuum of too little (most of us) to too much; explore hitting the sweet spot as The Real Me, player, in balance, day to day.

When you find yourself playing today, notice: Am I in flow? How does it feel?

As a child, I would often shrink from play, I was a somewhat serious and solitary child. I didn't like losing and was oddly competitive and unsocial, and so struggled to find the fun in playing. I wasn't physically gifted, couldn't throw, couldn't catch, and playing somehow made me feel stupid and 'less than'. I didn't like feeling stupid, so I simply avoided playing sports and games. And it was extra embarrassing because I would spontaneously burst into tears when struggling to play or performing badly.

My super-sporty, fun Mother often looked at me curiously, as if I'd been swapped at birth. Patiently, she taught me to tune into the fun of playing, simply *being with others* in whatever random activity was chosen. Understanding and experiencing the enjoyment of hanging with friends and family and not minding who wins. I learnt that games are not a reflection of one's intellect or prowess. Still, learning to play happily with little regard for outcomes has been a constant and personal companion to evolving my *Real Me*. Chess is still my Achilles heel. I play to challenge myself but when my 11-year-old daughter and 25-year-old son take my Queen in three moves, I still struggle.

The Real Me is a player, not to win and not to take advantage of others (though playing for money or buttons can be fun). And hey, if you can make a living through ethical and clever playing, go for it.

Tapping Into the Superpowers of The Real Me

"Nothing lights up the brain like play."
(Dr. Stuart Brown)

We are designed to play, not simply as children but all through our lives. How can I incorporate play into my life to 'refresh' *The Real Me*, regularly – or every day? Come up with one, two or three ways and play today!

Play Inquiry Questions: What's My Relationship With Play?

Q: Do I play?
Q: Do I consider myself a playful person or personality? Does this matter?
Q: What activities do I consider to be play for me? For others?
Q: To what extent do I value my own playtime?
Q: Do I suffer guilt when I play? (*"I should be doing..."*)
Q: If so, how do I alleviate this emotion or let it go? (Recognise, explore, allow, Let Go)
Q: Do I prefer to play alone or with others? (Give a ratio).
Q: What types of play do I fondly recall as a child?
Q: Do I seize opportunities to play with others - or does my ego/judgement say, *"I can't throw a ball, I'm hopeless"* or, *"I might lose the game"* and does this hinder my connection to playtime?
Q: How do I feel when I play? Before? During? After?
Q: How do I place myself on the play continuum? How does it feel to place myself there?

Never play _____ **my life is play**

(Unable to prioritize any play)   (Can't get my work done or care for myself)

The Real Me

Q: If I have children, do I join in with their play? Tea parties? Hot wheels? Computer games? Dress ups, rough and tumble, outside play, sporty play, arty play?
Q: If I have children, do I instigate play?
Q: Can I play respectfully, kindly and fairly, or do I get caught up in ego and being super competitive?
Q: Do I play to win to the point where I may have cheated?
Q: Can I celebrate others' achievements during play?
Q: Am I able to target playful friends to hang out with and play?
Q: What's my biggest (or top 3) barriers to play and how might I confront or soothe them?
Q: Can I *explore and find* elements of play in my work and relationships?
Q: Does my play generally have an agenda? If so, what? Hanging out with others, escape, stress release?
Q: Do I find myself in flow when playing?

Remember to come back to yourself, your heart and your light:

- If any of these questions triggered an unwelcome emotional reaction, breathe slowly and deeply for a minute or two, tuning yourself back into your body; smell or taste something, feel your feet on the ground or touch your clothes, stand, walk - bring yourself back into the moment.
- When you have the opportunity, write down the trigger question and allow the emotions to surface again; fear, powerlessness, regret, sadness; list them – and then tie into the powerful feeling of compassion – for yourself and any other person involved who was suffering and inflicting their pain on others.
- Stay with compassion until the emotions ebb away. Let go. Then move to the powerful feeling of forgiveness - for yourself, and any other person to release blame and guilt.

- Let go. Come back to yourself.

Exercise: Yes, have a play today. When coming into quiet breathwork and meditation, meditate on the word play, or a delightful playing experience you recall. Relax and enjoy.

Compassion; The Ultimate Expression of The Real Me

*"If you want others to be happy, practice compassion.
If you want to be happy, practice compassion."*
(Dalai Lama)

Today is Compassion Day.

Compassion is my number one Superpower. It has Latin roots and literally means *"to suffer together with another"* (Oxford). Researchers define it as, *"The feeling that arises when you are confronted with another's suffering* **and** *feel motivated to relieve that suffering"* (Berkeley, 2020). It's other-oriented feeling within ourselves. Compassion has a greater depth than empathy, in which you perceive and to some level, feel another's pain but are not necessarily motivated to render assistance.

Compassion has been measured via pupil dilation (and return) in children. Pupils dilate when the subject notices distress in others, and return to normal pupil size when the subject either decides they can assist, or when they observe assistance coming from another source. Fascinating.

While compassion may be viewed by some as a bleeding heart, irrational, pointless or perhaps a confronting feeling, research has shown that biologically, our heart rate slows, blood pressure drops, and we secrete the hormone oxytocin — otherwise known as the *"bonding"* or *"cuddle"* hormone and also released during hugs — when experiencing compassion. (Esch & Stefano, 2011) Sounds like flow? It does to me.

Areas of the brain engaged are pleasure centers and higher-level functions, including reward anticipation, impulse control, decision-making, and emotion.

Compassion hinges on *our ability* (and sensitivity) to recognise suffering in others and some assessment of our own ability to assist in some way. In addition, compassion can be broadened to include local and familial compassion, stranger compassion, and global compassion.

Compassion heals both the giver and recipient.

Compassion can sometimes be misinterpreted as a sign of weakness, especially if we were not raised to show compassion or in a non-compassionate household. It is not. Compassion is a sign of heartfelt connectedness. Being hard on others (grow a pair, toughen up) can indicate our own mirroring and that we struggle to show compassion for ourselves; generally because we were never taught or shown compassion or our compassion was mocked in some way. Research shows that compassion contributes to healing and resilience as well as healthy relationships and boundaries. Self-compassion reduces burnout, self-criticism, depression, PTSD symptoms as well as fostering positive experiences of aging and adaptivity. (Lonczak, 2020).

Compassion has its own kind of flow; you might consider it an energy which, like gratitude, works *The Real Me* on both the Compassionate and Compassioned, and flows out to others, paying it forward.

Compassion says *I see You.*

Compassion Exercises:

Spend a moment or better, a minute on each or any of these exercises:

- Imagine yourself sitting quietly with someone who really cares about you. Feel into the imagined experience.

- Spend a moment or minute sending compassion to someone who might need it; a prayer or imagined conversation or visualise a heart-to-heart transmission.

- Consider noticing when an opportunity for a word, act or gesture of compassion may arise in your day. Take the opportunity.

"Compassion brings inner peace and whatever else is going on, that peace of mind allows us to see the whole picture more clearly."
(Dalai Lama)

Compassion is a skill, and like any skill we can learn it and become more proficient with practise.

Compassion Inquiry Questions:
What's My Relationship With Compassion?

Q: What *is* my relationship with compassion?
Q: How does an act, word or gesture of compassion feel in my body? As I give? As I accept?
Q: As a child, did I witness compassion within my family? In which situations?

The Real Me

Q: If not, can I identify situations where more compassion might have helped me to live my life as *The Real Me*?
Q: Am I kind to myself? How have I learned this?
Q: Do I extend compassion more easily to others than to myself?
Q: When I'm flat, tired, anxious, or depressed, am I able to show compassion to myself? In which ways?
Q: Can I demonstrate honor to the experiences of myself or others when in distress?
Q: Do I soothe and care for myself and others when in distress? Even when I'm not sure what to do?
Q: What actions do I take to bring comfort, peace, relief or joy to myself or others in moments of suffering?
Q: Do I accept pain as part of the shared human experience?
Q: Do I connect with others through the common experiences of suffering?
Q: In which situations might I be unkind to myself? Take a moment to explore this one. Is this learned? Can I recognise, explore, allow and let it go?
Q: What motivates me to connect compassionately with others?
Q: Am I interested in the welfare of other beings? My immediate family? People I know? My ethnic group particularly? People with beliefs very different to mine? Animals and plants? Our planet?
Q: Is there ever hesitation to extend compassion towards myself or others? In which situations?
Q: Do I shut down compassion to myself or others as a coping mechanism? Because I think they are wrong? Because I don't know how to help myself, let alone others? Because I simply can't bear the pain of others?
Q: What might be some boundaries of my compassion?

Self-Compassion Exercise:
If you noticed heavier feelings, darker colours or lower numbers around the inquiry questions around *self-compassion*, here's

Tapping Into the Superpowers of The Real Me

a beautiful exercise by Kristin Neff that you might like to work through. Give yourself around half an hour for this one; it can be transformative and very healing: *(Italics are by Sarah).*

1. Try thinking about an issue that tends to make you feel inadequate or bad about yourself (e.g. physical appearance, work or relationship issues). How does this aspect of yourself make you feel inside - scared, sad, depressed, insecure, or angry? What emotions come up for you when you think about this aspect of yourself? Please try to be as emotionally honest as possible and to avoid repressing any feelings, while at the same time not being melodramatic. Try to just feel your emotions exactly as they are - nothing more, nothing less. *(Even if you are unable to give words to the emotions).*

2. Now think about an imaginary friend who is unconditionally loving, accepting, kind, and compassionate. Imagine that this friend can see all your strengths and all your weaknesses, including the aspect of yourself you have just been thinking about. Reflect upon what this friend feels toward you, and how you are loved and accepted exactly as you are, with all your very human imperfections. This friend recognises the limits of human nature and is kind and forgiving toward you. In their great wisdom, this friend understands your life history and the millions of things that have happened in your life to create you as you are in this moment. *(I love this).*

   Your particular inadequacy is connected to so many things you didn't necessarily choose: your genes, your family history, life circumstances - things that were outside of your control. Write a letter to yourself from the perspective of this imaginary friend - focusing on the perceived inadequacy you tend to judge yourself for. What would this friend say to you about your *"flaw"* from the perspective of unlimited compassion? How would this friend convey the deep compassion they feel for you, especially for the discomfort you feel when you judge yourself so harshly? What would this friend write in order to remind you that you are only human, that all people have both strengths and weaknesses? And if you think this friend would suggest possible changes you should make; how would these suggestions embody feelings of unconditional understanding and compassion? As you write to yourself from the perspective of this imaginary friend, try to infuse your letter with a strong sense of the person's acceptance, kindness, caring, and desire for your health and happiness.

3. After writing the letter, put it down for a little while. Then come back and read it again, really letting the words sink in. Feel the compassion as it pours into you, soothing and comforting you like a cool breeze on a hot day.

> *"Love, connection, and acceptance are your birthright. To claim them you need only look within yourself."*
> (Kristin Neff, Self-Compassion: Stop Beating Yourself Up and Leave Insecurity Behind)

The Real Me is compassionate.
Is this an area of The Real Me that you've buried deep or armoured up to avoid hurt? Would you like to explore and practise more compassion in your daily life? Today is Compassion Day. Look for moments today to notice compassion, extend compassion, and support the compassion shown by others. Notice what you notice, observe any emotions and how compassion feels in your body. Notice any questions around compassion; an answer may well arise.

Tapping Into the Superpowers of The Real Me

Exercise: During your quiet moments of Self practise today, consider meditating on Compassion or an element of compassion which has emerged for your attention today.

> *"Compassion is not only relevant to those who are blameless victims, but also to those whose suffering stems from failures, personal weakness, or bad decisions. You know, the kind **you and I** make every day."*
> *(Kristin Neff)*

Curiosity - Inquiry *Is* a Superpower

> *"The important thing is not to stop questioning. Curiosity has its own reason for existing. One cannot help but be in awe when he contemplates the mysteries of eternity, of life, of the marvellous structure of reality. It is enough if one tries merely to comprehend a little of this mystery every day."*
> *(Albert Einstein)*

Today is Curiosity Day.

We are born asking why? Curiosity gets our chin up looking around; curiosity is exploring, curiosity is inquiring, it sees us bouncing ourselves off our world and noticing what we don't yet understand. It's not knowing quite what the day will bring. The power of curiosity gets children out of bed in the morning. What are we doing today? What will we see? What might happen? What will I discover? What will I enjoy?

Who will be there with *Me*?

The Real Me

What gets Me out of bed in the morning?

Curiosity taps into the great unknown and is a Superpower of *The Real Me*. It is defined as being eager to know, learn or experience something. *The Real Me* is insatiably curious. The exhausted, overwhelmed, anxious, depressed or too comfortable *Me* is not. Notice this in yourself. Curiosity takes *The Real Me* to the next level.

Curiosity is noticing something that we find interesting.

When we are curious, we are in the moment and have shaken off our *"all in the mind"*, grey fugue. We want to see, We want to know, We want to connect; *Now*!

A USC study on curiosity has shown that curious toddlers have a significant IQ lead by age 11, than less curious toddlers. In addition, curious 60-86-year-old subjects were more likely to be alive five years beyond their less curious counterparts - even when smoking and health issues were considered.

I like Wikipedia's definition: *"Curiosity is a quality related to inquisitive thinking such as exploration, investigation, and learning, evident by observation in humans and other animals. Curiosity is heavily associated with all aspects of human development, in which derives the process of learning and desire to acquire knowledge and skill."*

This entire course is built on the premise of your curiosity about yourself, your life; how you engage with each moment and 'show up.' Being curious about yourself is a way of relating to your highest destiny path within each and every moment of your life.

Curiosity Inquiry Questions:
What Is My Relationship With Curiosity?

Q: Do I consider myself curious? Make a shortlist of the questions, topics or activities, sights or sounds which spark your curiosity. Keep coming back to this list and adding to it during today.
Q: Can I, or do I inspire curiosity in others? Model curiosity for others?
Q: Can I interrogate tasks I have judged as mundane, boring, or repetitive and look for elements of interest I have missed?
Q: Do I ask questions of others?
Q: What do I want to know *in this moment* that I could find out?
Q: Do I experience curiosity fatigue - there is so much to find out and so much internet to surf that it's dulled my experience of curiosity?
Q: Am I somewhat fearful of curiosity? Why might this be?
Q: Do I *"hate surprises"* yet tell stories (and am proud of) of how I responded to particular unexpected events?
Q: Can I encourage curiosity in my co-workers? My family? *The Real Me*?

What *Really* Interests Me? In a series of emails, or social media posts, which posts pique my interest to open first? This brings us back to the first **Q** above and can inform about what we really love to do in our lives, our passions and connections, where we find our flow and how we like to share and express ourselves.

Curiosity is a key to The Real Me.

The Real Me is a curious *Me*. What really interests you, that you can investigate today? Can you share your interest and findings with others?

The Real Me

The Real Me is fully connected with the energies and values of play, gratitude, courage, curiosity and compassion.

Exercise.

Q: Where's my curiosity at?

Ask the Question and give yourself a moment. Notice what comes up. Words, a number or %, a feeling.

Set yourself the task of being curious today. It may be asking a co-worker or family member a question about them that you really want to know. Or finding a patch of grass, lifting a dead leaf and examining the microcosm of life there for a minute. Or googling something you've wondered about, tasting something new or listening to an emerging artist.

Q: How do I feel in those moments where I am engaging with curiosity. Flow?

How was your Curiosity Day? What did you discover? About yourself? Meditate today on Curiosity and it those few quiet moments, what do you really want to find out, explore, create and discover as *The Real Me*?

"I am not afraid. I was born to do this."
(Joan of Arc)

Courage - Discretion Is a Virtue, Courage Is Your Superpower

"Fear is a reaction, courage is a decision."
(Winston Churchill)

It's Courage Day today. Take a breath. Let's explore courage together.

Oxford defines Courage as the ability to do something that frightens one; bravery *and* strength in the face of pain or grief.

Let's consider courage as a continuum and as a choice resulting in action (or mindful inaction) with reaction or fearful action/inaction at the opposite end.

Living each day as *The Real Me* gives ample opportunities to display and choose Courage. Plus there are many forms of courage; incarnations if you like. Courage will have very different personal actions and applications to you, compared with family, friends and others. Can you relate to the courage it takes to ('simply') get out of bed some mornings? To speak up when a person at work is suffering verbal abuse? To offer to help another when you don't have a clue what to do? To join a team when you believe your lack of skills may cause your team a handicap? To turn up to class every day feeling you're simply not good enough? These are some of my personal examples. Write down some of your own.

Is there a difficult conversation you've been putting off? Part of a creative project you've been nervous to tackle? Today is the Day!

Courage is the decision to choose to act as The Real Me in any situation.

The Real Me

Courage Questions: What's My Relationship with Courage?

Bring to mind a situation where I feel I displayed courage.
Q: How did I feel prior to choosing courage?
Q: How did I feel in the midst of performing/speaking courageously?
Q: How did I feel immediately afterwards? hours later? days later?
Q: Do I consider myself courageous?
Q: Do I consider courage to be folly? Putting myself in harm's way?
Q: Do I consider courage to be a virtue of value to *The Real Me*, and continually practise courage and flex my 'courage muscles'? Place myself on the courage continuum. Is this where The Real Me might place myself?

Courageous _____ **fearful**
(Acting from my values)   (Inaction or not acting from values)

Q: Can I name 3 role models I consider to be courageous? Explore.
Q: Can I name situations in which I display courage? Situations in which I back away from courage?
Q: Do I display courage in the face of unkindness to myself? Others?
Q: Do I find courage stimulating or exhausting? Can I explore a balance point, today?
Q: Can courage be choosing to refrain, not act, in a given situation?

Exercise: Take some time today to meditate on courage. Simply on the word, Courage. Find opportunities within your Courage Day to be courageous in moments, little or large. What was one situation today I expressed *The Real Me* through courageous action or mindful inaction?

The Real Me is fully connected with the energies and values of beauty, play, courage, curiosity and compassion.

The Real Me is emerging, open and grateful.

Tapping Into the Superpowers of The Real Me

The Real Me is so excited to be here, with you, in this moment!

"People grow through experiences if they meet life honestly and courageously. This is how character is built."

"We gain courage and wisdom from every instance in which we stop to look fear in the face."
(Eleanor Roosevelt)

Chapter 7 has encompassed huge chunks of exploration. Take a break if you need to or expand over a couple of weeks. If you find yourself greying out over too many inquiry questions, pick three at random, or by choice, from each list and really sit with them. You can ask the questions during your breathing and meditation practises to allow them to soak in deep. Notice your responses in any feeling or imagery that arises. Take it slow, and remember, you can't do it wrong. Just Do It!

Exercise: Write Your Own Questions!

We've explored some of the areas of the 90% of our lives that are invisible in this chapter, and those which I feel are the top 6 Superpowers of *The Real Me*. If there is a Superpower we haven't covered together that you're called to explore, (I wish she'd done Honesty or Trust, Integrity, Values, Love, Hope, Inspiration, Wisdom), or your particular other, tune into *The Real Me* and write some questions for yourself. You can model them on the style of Q in this book or allow them to come up in free writing.

Before you begin, do your breathing and meditation exercises to calm your mind. This helps you reach within and connect with your

The Real Me

Real Me, (not your mind, *The Real Me* is infinitely more!) Simple Questions that come from a place of both knowing and wanting to experience & explore will arise. You will only know *through* experiencing them. Respond to your questions in your own time. You may often find that the response comes up with the question, almost concurrently.

Now, to the Dark Side.

Chapter 8

Entering the Dagobah Cave; Lighting the Dark Corners of The Real Me

> *"There are things we don't know we don't know."*
> *(Donald Rumsfeld)*

The things we don't know we don't know *are the buried me, the submerged part of our iceberg. They can be Dark and invisible,* even to ourselves.

Moving from the great champions of *The Real Me*, Week 8 takes us into the dark side. Each day, set aside a few moments to connect with yourself via breath and meditation. Keep focusing on *choice*; every moment, notice, unlearn and re-learn. Allow being and seeing *Me* to be a priority.

The Real Me

You might already have noticed some changes in the way you are expressing yourself, *The Real Me*, Right Now in the outside world and in your life. Other people might be responding to you slightly differently; they've noticed, and *you've* noticed. Perhaps you've become aware of how hard, but also how simple self-realization really is. It's a whole series of seeing with new eyes, and noticing the way you respond. The beauty of *The Real Me* process is that you're not having to do/change/force anything that isn't already there.

You might resonate with the metaphor of an unconscious clay figurine or toy waking and coming to life. *You* are the most (spiritually and soulfully) aware and advanced that you've ever been *Right Now*; right in this moment. And if you've been following the exercises in this book, you'll have some sense of where you are on this journey. Work with your favourite superpowers this week, especially compassion and gratitude, as well as your own creativity activities. Practise Recognising, Exploring, Allowing and Letting go as we enter the Cave.

The dark corners of The Real Me are not our foes; rather they are our greatest teachers.

Our personal Cave holds some of our most deeply held unconscious beliefs. These have been absorbed into us from our external environments, caregivers and society, some certainly well meaning. They are our scaffolding views about the world we live in, about money, about ourselves, others and how others relate to us. Many of these core beliefs were formed when we were very young, thus may have a simple, childlike quality to them. Trauma will create or distort other unconscious beliefs. We don't challenge them because

    a. we don't know they are there, and
    b. they have masqueraded as our truths.

Entering the Dagobah Cave

Yet they may not be our *Real* Truths. Some are our blind spots, they keep us down, they have held us back, they are disabling. They keep us bound and worse, gagged. They are beliefs that we don't know we believe but affect and underpin our choices and our actions. These unconscious, sub-conscious core beliefs are like *"pay no attention to that man behind the curtain"* in *The Wizard of Oz*; directing our experiences and choices without our direct awareness; lenses through we perceive ourselves, the world; everything. Take a moment to consider this truth at your deepest level.

Yet there *are* things we notice when an unconscious, un-True belief system is operating. These are feelings of contraction and smallness; closed and heaviness, fear, doubt, regret, shame and unworthiness. Remember, the most genuine parts of *The Real Me* **are** invisible. They are qualities of our authentics truths and not sullied by our life experiences. They are our most intrinsic and real values, often hidden, buried *and unrealised.*

Our logical mind does and will continue to struggle to understand the vastness of our true nature. Many of these un-True beliefs are like concrete or armour around our hearts. They are familiar, so are unchallenged. These layers result in *The Real Me* being unable to flow out and be seen; to be experienced by ourselves and others and compromise our being *Real* in each moment.

Remember too that your thinking mind works with learned algorithms it's created, based on what it has already experienced; it takes time to explore, create & strengthen neural pathways for new ideas so be gentle and open. Consider how un-examined, unconscious beliefs *"running the show"* might not only be true for you, but also others around you. Be compassionate.

The Real Me

In working with The Real Me course thus far, you've observed and shifted some of the stuff that's not really you. Now we're going deeper.

An example from my own experience is the unconscious belief that (my) romantic relationship will work, as long as I try hard enough and sacrifice enough and believe (yes, *believe!*) it will work. There was a lot about relationships I didn't understand. I didn't know what I didn't know, and I couldn't see it. There was a distinct pattern in all my relationships ending with me being dumped. In one particular relationship - and after a pivotal conversation with my son at the washing line, *"Mum, do you really want the rest of your life to be like this?"* - I actually experienced the scales falling from my eyes and something inside me opened and released. I think I physically started to shake and nearly fell over. The understanding burst outwards from within me that:

"I don't want to do this anymore."

I experienced a completely new understanding and a change of heart, almost like a Matrix-style software upgrade. A belief I didn't even know I believed simply fell away, leaving an incredible feeling of freedom. I suddenly understood that I can't fix everything, I can't control all outcomes, not all relationships are forever and it's okay. I'm okay. I don't have to perpetuate or save a failing relationship to be a good or worthy person.

> *"'What is in the cave, Master Yoda?' Yoda responds, 'Only what you take with you.'"*
> *(Episode V: The Empire Strikes Back)*

The five biggest blocks to fully becoming *The Real Me* in this lifetime are:

Entering the Dagobah Cave

1. Ignorance: The Veil; you don't know what you don't know.
2. Fear and doubt: The Undertakers; they bury The Real Me deep and are the primordial contracting emotions; shutting *The Real Me* down at every opportunity.
3. Ease: The Lull; like the stories of Pleasure Island in *"Pinocchio,"* all is not as it seems...
4. Words: The Rose or the Club; our ideas and beliefs are often framed and encapsulated in our words, the meaning we ascribe to them, how we choose to use them and our interpretation of the words of others.
5. Clutter: The Burden; where is *The Real Me* amongst all of this?

We're going to explore them one by one, this week. Breathe and receive; take a few paragraphs of encouragement and light:

Be gentle with yourself today and every day moving forward. When you're writing in your journal, write one, two, or three things down that you've noticed today. Maybe you've have had a big *"aha!"* moment. A full blast of enlightenment in some way. Perhaps, you've had more than one. Perhaps you're having them every day - though for most of us, it's the little *"aha's!"* that bring us ever more into our own light.

*Awareness **is** the great light.*

Come back to *The Real Me*, just as you are, *Right Now*. Believe that coming back to the Real MeRightNow is always the biggest gain you can make.

Visualize an image of *Me*, a relaxed and expansive figure on the edge of a light beam and occasionally, plunging into greater illumination. Breathe and notice our human tendency to be dismissive of our own gains and impatient for the next, so take a moment to simply smile, relax and celebrate *Me*. It's a natural human trait to see the mountains before us as huge, and those we've already climbed as *"Oh, that was nothing"* - though it most certainly was at the time!

One of the boons of journaling is to simply look back from time to time and see how *far* you've come, and the insights you've had; the newly discovered joys, paths and *Self*.

During a meditation session with Swami Jasraj Puri, we were invited to perform a reflective meditation - to take ourselves mentally backward through our day, bringing to mind the tasks we performed, the emotions we experienced, and to notice when the mind alights and what it dwells upon. A few days later, my friend Nuria, remarked that she wasn't able to drop easily to sleep that night as she had a major realisation of just how much she'd done in that one day. She'd experienced a powerful level of surprise and shock at the number of tasks achieved in a single day and was still reeling from it. Possibly, her realisation was her own personal power to make things happen; perhaps it was the necessity to slow down, and really extract meaning from all the experiences of one day.

Remember that the process of allowing *The Real Me* to emerge into your own life, and the lives of those around you, is a long and winding road with stops and starts. Take it at your pace.

Pre-Cave Practise: Releasing and Letting go

This is possibly the most important practice in the Real Me course, particularly if you have suffered intense & difficult experiences, trauma or have developed habitual negativity.

Entering the Dagobah Cave

Before we enter the Cave, we'll take 5 minutes to re-visit our REAL acronym from Chapter 2. You may have been using this daily and have personalised it to suit your experiences. You may have forgotten it! It doesn't matter. Notice when little things bring up large responses. Notice when you feel dark, heavy and contracted throughout this week. Small and heavy is never the real You. Come back to REAL:

- ✓ Recognise and Experience (emotions, physical sensations, non-smooth breath). Explore.
- ✓ Allow and Let go.

Exercise:

If you've ever read or been told to 'Let It Go' and wondered exactly how to do it, this is it. Below is a useful practise for letting go, and as with all our work, feel free to customise as to what works for you; you'll know via practise and *experience*.

The Real Me practice is letting go in action, releasing Unreal parts of MeRightNow and unfolding your Real Me in the moment.

Bring to mind an unpleasant situation where you lost control; you yelled or were yelled at, you were frightened or embarrassed or someone else dumped their shit on you and in your surprise or blindside, you accepted it on some level. Skip this exercise right now if it's too confronting or choose a yellow situation rather than full red. *'Why would I want to 'relive' this?'* It's the only way to release it. We're practising! Choose.

Sit or lie down if you are standing. Or pace/walk if you prefer. Immerse yourself in this chosen awful situation. When you notice yourself there, breathe. Notice your breath. Notice physical sensations. Notice thoughts but don't engage in *the* story you're telling yourself nor any kind of blame.

Notice that you are feeling safe, and with absolute presence, hold the space. Hold the space and breathe. Hold the space and breathe.

Begin to notice your breath gradually slow and become more regular. Feel into your compassion for yourself in this moment as well as *that* moment. You may be able to feel compassion for another who was involved and not behaving as their Real Me. Stay here for around 5 minutes or until your breath is smooth and your physical symptoms subside.

If you choose, you can call in The Light and feel white light washing over and through you as if it was poured on your head from an endless bucket, flowing around your body and through your body. If this seems weird and new-agey, simply trial it and allow. Feel it flowing through each cell, radiating out through your fingertips and toes. Continue cleansing with light for 5 breaths or as long as feels right. You may feel yourself seamlessly settle into meditation or breath-work for a few minutes. When you are ready,

Q: How am I feeling, mind breath and body, right now?

You may feel calm and light, you may feel odd, queasy or exhausted and need to sleep or rest. You may feel balanced, or strange and not find the words. Equally you may feel some residual emotion, perhaps anger, sadness, blankness, numbness or other. Remember, you can't do it wrong and some healing will take many sessions. Be gentle and compassionate. Only you can do this work. If you can, journal your experience.

Entering the Dagobah Cave

You'll know if you need this practice. If so, complete this practise every day for a week to tweak and make this practise your own. You can work formally and sit down with the darkness you've chosen or already experienced and/or practise in day to day confronting moments as they arise. Ideally both. This practise is transformative and allows you to build some muscle memory, emotional memory, intellectual memory and breath memory of this practise of letting go. You will find your Way, your own process of letting go of chunks of MeRightNow which you begin to recognise as *not The Real Me*.

So, this is what it *is*: The chunky, sometimes uncomfortable part of noticing every moment *is* noticing: what you're doing and how you're feeling; noticing your breath and how it feels in your body; noticing emotions as well as physical sensations and holding the space in the present. It's about allowing release and healing to happen. It's about being Open to *The Real Me* in each moment. It is all about creating the safe space for your emotions to be acknowledged and ultimately resolved *whilst being with* whatever is occurring in the moment.

A Whole me is a Healed me and The Real Me

And this is what it's *not*: It's not being attached to the dark experience and re-living it over and over with the same pain and no change. It's not routinely and mindlessly, habitually applying negative patterns, attributes and thoughts.

It's about noticing any uncomfortable, negative, closed and heavy sensations or thoughts that arise, but choosing **not** to automatically distract myself, hide, yell or reach for my favourite dulling agent. Choosing not to apply something like alcohol, self-criticism or negativity to it.

The Real Me

Being The Real Me is being with whatever is happening in the story of you in the moment.

Dichotomy of Ease – The Lull

"Oh, you want an easy life?
I hear McDonalds is hiring."
(Harvey Spector, Suits)

This corner of our Cave invites us into Ease.

Today is our day to explore Easy.

> *"We choose to go to the Moon in this decade and do the other things, not because they are easy, but because they are hard; because that goal will serve to organize and measure the best of our energies and skills, because that challenge is one that we are willing to accept, one we are unwilling to postpone."*
> *(JFK)*

Our comfort zone is a safe place, but is it *too* safe? Are we denying ourselves opportunities to explore, be curious, challenged, and grow into *The Real Me*?

We're given numerous opportunities each day to Helicopter-parent ourselves.

Let's shift away from this temptation to Nanny ourselves, and towards dissecting and understanding the pervasive marketing and subtle inundation of the concepts of ease and comfort into our lives. Yeah, that can be a tricky one because ease is a big marketing

Entering the Dagobah Cave

tool: *"Let's make this easy, honestly, my method/device/app makes your life easier."* You know the drill.

Consider all those "time-saving" apps you never use and devices and appliances you have in the backs of cupboards. And when the dishwasher is stacked and switched on, how do we use the time we've freed? Yes, we might well be playing guitar, board games with the kids, creating, chatting with friends or relaxing. But are we?

Ease can be defined as an absence of difficulty or effort, freedom from worries or problems, a release of tension but also, to move gradually or carefully; as in to Ease our way into something. We can use the term to intuit our ability or willingness to tackle a physical challenge – an easy hiking trail or some level of physical fitness! What's your relationship with Ease?

Comfort is the result of an *application of ease* either physically, or emotionally. We can provide comfort by easing the pain of another or ourselves. Easing into comfort can be a magical moment, but do we ever find ourselves seeking ease for ease's own sake, rather than focusing life around our curiosity, finding our flow and our creative journey? Deferring to ease, rather than choosing or accepting our challenges according to *The Real Me*? Choosing comfort over interest? Choosing avoidance, over feeling fully alive?

In this moment, start exploring, and identify an area in your life where the fully engaged *Real Me* is completely absent, buried or ignored. What is coming up for you?

In states of being overwhelmed, exhausted, chronic illness or fear, we sometimes run, rage, or cry, but equally, we may succumb to boredom, greying out and disengagement. None of these states are *The Real Me*. *The Real Me* loves a challenge and to learn new

The Real Me

things. *The Real Me* is insatiably curious, vulnerable, loving, and lovable, energised yet relaxed. So, let's explore the continuum and dichotomy of Ease:

Ease is not a purpose.

Comfort and ease have a definite and valued place in our balanced lives, though not at the forefront. When we are in flow state, our body feels energized but relaxed. Not tense. In flow, we find the balance of effort and Ease.

Remember when Dorothy and her friends set out for Oz? Yep. Another parable about the journey to find *The Real Me*. Dorothy was sabotaged when led into the poppy field. She was on her way to Oz; a path to home. We can relate. Dorothy and friends were overcome with stupor, forgot their path and settled in for an easy sleep. We too can quite easily sink into oblivion, doped, and sleepwalking. We just keep doing what we're already doing - that's called inertia. It's familiar; we don't have to subject ourselves to the sometimes-frightening notion of yet more change.

Visualize a rut. Following that rutted path doesn't bring us any closer to Oz, or our *Real Selves*. Change must not be forced and is not necessary for change's sake, but it must not be avoided or abandoned through fear or because *it's too hard*. Change, death, and taxes are constant and reliable, and change *will* happen to us if we don't happen to it.

Allow challenges to be appropriate and a good fit within your creativity, curiosity, and playfulness. Then they will feel right to *The Real Me,* even if we can't intellectually understand or foresee every part or bend in the road of our emerging scenario. If the next yellow brick appears before us, we step. If our attention is drawn to a scarecrow off the yellow brick road, we explore, rather than stay on the road out of fear or habit.

The Real Me philosophy is that we walk the path that's right, energetically, for *Me* within the continuum of effort and Ease. If something's too easy, it's like falling into the poppies and going to sleep and life goes on around us and we're somnambulating through life, not really engaging as *The Real Me*. We become dissatisfied on some levels, and we intuitively know it. Perhaps it manifests as depression, anxiety or anger and none of these states are the real you.

Occasionally, we might pop up and engage – think meerkat! – and then sink back down again. Spend some time this week noticing when and what things in your life may be too easy, and what things; note when things in your life seem overwhelming or too hard. Then consider how you respond to this. Ask yourself these inquiry questions and listen to what comes up:

Q: What does the word *"easy"* feel like in my body when I say it to myself? Light or heavy? What about *"comfort"* and *"simple"*.
Q: What is my language around ease? Generally positive or suspicious: *"Thanks, that's easy!"* or *"Easy? I don't' think so!"*
Q: Am I always looking for or attracted to easy? Explore.
Q: Are there areas in which I choose ease instead of growth? What are they? Why might that be?
Q: Can I articulate reasons for pursuing ease? Journal them.
Q: Can I define my relationship with easy?
Q: Am I pursuing ease to release more time for nourishing activities or rest?
Q: Does easy work for me when I investigate it for myself, rather than others pushing it on me?
Q: Do I fear challenge as it might make me look foolish or unskilled or vulnerable in front of others?

The Real Me

Q: Do I fear ease as it might make me look lazy in front of others?
Q: Do I like creating ease; i.e. simpler methods or items because others can benefit?
Q: Can I explore the ease and challenge dichotomy in each moment and live life in flow, as *The Real Me*?

On one hand, Ease is a beautiful gift we like to extend to others in a moment of flow, grace or compassion: *"Here, let me show you; let me do this for you."* Those moments when someone shows you a more straightforward way of completing a task - and you get it - is wonderful. For me, it's when my daughter finds my glasses for me, or my son teaches me a simpler *"C chord"* on the guitar. It is a gift we can accept when tired and overwhelmed, or through careful choice.

The other end of the spectrum, an Easy life can be an un-engaged, un-examined existence where keeping the Status Quo becomes and end in itself rather than living; playing it safe and taking the easy path, rather than asking the important questions which propel us into the unknown. A Life of Ease can ensure we never show up as the Real Me.

> *"It is an invitation to live life fully and completely, which is never ultimately safe and is often uncomfortable."*
> *(Gangaji)*

Spend time today exploring Ease in all its manifestations with the goal of finding balance. Meditate on the delights of both Ease and challenge. Find your place on the continuum.

Entering the Dagobah Cave

Ignorance – The Veil

Ignorance might be bliss but it's not The Real Me.

Today is Ignorance Day. Let's explore.

We don't see reality, rather we see what we think is reality, both in ourselves, our relationships and the world around us. Each of us has hundreds of perceptions of what the world is like, entirely constructed of *our own* past experiences, habits, expectations, judgments and beliefs.

Let's briefly revisit Chapter 2. The idea that our entire life and world concept being created by our minds might immediately raise red flags. Each of us, via our own reality, have created our own realities!

> *"We see the world not as it is but as we are."*
> *(Anais Nin)*

Intellectually, we may not grasp this, so simply consider it. We observe this Deep Truth in simple or dramatic scenarios when, after together experiencing the same event or idea with others, we have opposing or markedly different recounts. Our lens of life, the Universe and everything is unique to us.

We have spent most of our lives believing that our thoughts are truth, our perceptions are reality, and that what we individually believe is "right" is the truth. This ignorance can be most difficult to overcome due to our habitual patterns of thinking. Our questions this week will shine a light into those dark places, and simply bring awareness to not just how much there is to learn and experience being *The Real Me*, but because there's a great deal to un-learn, chip away, let go and release as we recover *The Real Me*.

The Real Me

*You've noticed that inquiry **Q** are hard. It's easier to read a question and move on than it is to really enquire. Keep challenging yourself:*

Q: Who do I think I am? Take a few moments to write down the first things that pop into your head – it might be your work, profession, values or qualities you associate with yourself.

Q: Who might I be without any (or all) of the above?

Q: What's one story I tell about myself which isn't true? Why? Unpack this a little further. Perhaps work on another, then another or choose a time to revisit.

Q: Which personal traits do I exhibit which are really not me? Perhaps I've outgrown them or grown used to them – *or other people expect them of me*?

Q: Which issues do I deal with on a regular basis which aren't *The Real Me* – addictions, family dramas, conflict, self doubt, _____ , _____?

Q: Do I associate my happiness with a particular person?

Q: Do I associate my self-worth with a particular outcome? In which situations?

Q: Am I able to re-examine long standing views with openness and self-compassion?

Q: Has a long-standing habit plastered over my openness to new ideas or choices?

Q: Do I have traits of stubbornness or perceived intellectual ability which I can explore?

Q: Do I feel stuck or helpless, lacking ideas or motivation to move in a different direction?

Q: Do I perceive a lack of will or skill on my part to nudge out of my comfort zone?

Q: Do I mistake/accept lies for truth in the pursuit of the status quo?

Q: Do I mistake suffering for joy when analyzing some of my choices? Why might this be?

Entering the Dagobah Cave

Q: Which type(s) of ignorance in others bother me most? How do I respond?

> *"Any moment that causes us to question our assumptions about reality has the potential to lift our veil."*
> *(Sally Kempton)*

Spend time today exploring Ignorance, your Core beliefs and areas where an expanded Real Me is waiting to emerge. Meditate on releasing ignorance and tuning in to *The Real Me*.

Clutter – The Burden

> *"Clear clutter —make space for YOU."*
> *(Magdelena Vandenberg)*

Today is Clutter Day. There's a feeling of dread and doom stealing over me as I write this. Letting go....Let's explore.

Clutter is the adversary of space and a spacious me is *The Real Me*.

Clutter is defined as *"a lot of things in an untidy state, things that are not useful"* (Collins) or to *"cover or fill with an untidy collection of things"* (Oxford). Harsh. My definition of clutter goes further and my personal relationship with clutter is one not yet resolved. My definition is that clutter:

1. Comprises of physical, emotional, and energetic stuff we've *collected and accepted.* Purposely or unwittingly.
2. May be meticulously catalogued and stored but is still clutter.
3. Has expired in its relevance.

4. Feels heavy and burdensome both in mind and body.
5. Does not reflect *The Real Me*.

Physical Clutter: For those of us living in relative Western abundance, clutter reflects our society's values and pervasiveness of advertising. *Home Beautiful* magazines and furniture catalogues show clear, spartan, light rooms; styled to attract the spaciousness of The Real Me observer. *Our rooms* look somewhat different.

Emotional Clutter: Most of us carry some level of emotional clutter in our bodies and our energetic being. Think of a time when you were emotionally hurt, in pain or suffered and, there it is. It's difficult to pinpoint just where in our bodies it's lurking and stuck, but release and let go at any time you *feel* it. This practise will begin to soften, shift energetic clutter and allow it fall away, leaving a bright, clear *Real Me*. Be patient, notice and allow it to happen. Work with the Letting go practise; keep bringing it to the surface of your awareness, holding space, breathing and releasing.

Scientific and psychological study shows links between physical clutter and:

- Life dissatisfaction
- Increased levels of cortisol (stress hormone); particularly in women - surprise, surprise!
- Decreased immune response quality
- Increased anxiety levels
- Decreased sleep quality
- Lowering of ability to focus
- Reduction in working memory
- Shrinkage in the ability to process information
- Less clarity in the interpretation of emotions in faces of others
- Issues with maintaining normal weight

Entering the Dagobah Cave

Research has shown that being in a messy room will make you twice as likely to reach for a chocolate bar than an apple! On the other hand, another study showed messy desks can lead us into more creativity, whereas neat and orderly desk users were more likely to conform and play it safe. (Vohs, Redden & Rahinel.) Consider how these studies may relate to you.

Marie Kondo's *KonMari* method was trending a couple of years ago; there are plenty of methodologies available for those whose home organization doesn't reflect *The Real Me*. Remember, it's all about perception and *The Real Me*; everyone's idea of clutter will be different and may evolve as *The Real Me* emerges.

Today's inquiry questions unpack where you are with clutter: Come back to relaxed breathing if some questions trigger an emotional response.

Q: How do you feel in mind and body simply in the presence of the word Clutter and reading the last paragraphs? Any tension? Laugh-out-louds?
Q: What's your personal definition of clutter? Draft and re-draft it.
Q: Do you feel spacious and 'at home' in your home? If not, can you explain why without blame?
Q: Do you need to move things in order to work at your workspace?
Q: Do you consider space, storage area, maintenance and general use when you buy or accept an item into your home?
Q: Are you (like me) an energetic magnet for people's old clothes and things? (they just turn up at your house)?
Q: Do you have a storage space (sheds, spare rooms) which fit the Oxford definition of clutter?
Q: Will you refuse to part with outdated or unused items 'because you paid good money for them' or 'it might come in handy'?

The Real Me

Q: Do you feel emotionally attached to so many items that your friends would describe you as a hoarder? Ask a friend you know would be honest with you.
Q: Does clutter upset you?
Q: Do you ever buy an item because you can't find the ones you know you already have?
Q: Do you become overwhelmed by too many items/words/things in your field of vision?
Q: Is your or someone else's desk or workspace the 'nightmare' health hazard?
Q: Is your tidy desk or workspace a reflection of The Real Me or your perceiving of other's expectations/ judgments of you?
Q: Which element of clutter bothers you most? Rank from 1-5:
   a. *Other people's judgments.*
   b. *My own emotions of failure in some way.*
   c. *Waste of money & resources in all this unnecessary stuff.*
   d. *General responsibility for creating this situation.*
   e. *General responsibility for having to deal with the situation.*
   f. *The notion I've defined myself and my life via this stuff.*
   g. *No space! I need space!*
Q: Are you able to visualize a cluttered space without clutter?
Q: Is your schedule cluttered, leaving no time or space for yourself to breathe?

Today may not be the day to de-clutter but it can be the day to consider your relationship to clutter and create the beginnings of a shift.

My environment isn't an extension of me; my environment IS me.

Entering the Dagobah Cave

The Real Me is open and spacious.

> *"What makes a fire burn is space between the logs, a breathing space."*
> *(Judy Brown)*

Spend time today exploring Clutter in all its manifestations in your life with the goal of finding space. Space to live and breathe. Meditate on the delights of space, Openness and release.

Fear and Doubt – The Undertakers

> *"The Opposite of Love Is Not Hate, It's Fear."*
> *(Paulo Friere)*

Today we're exploring our relationships with Fear and Doubt. It's Fear Day.

For a moment, think of something which frightens you; or feign a fearful thought. Notice what happens to your body, to your breath. Ragged gulp of air or hardly breathing? Heart pumping, dilated pupils, physical tension, or tingles from head to toe... Definitely not the relaxed, flowing, focused *Real Me*!

As we know, thoughts affect our biology, and our biology returns the favour. Fearful, anxious thoughts trigger our sympathetic nervous system – fight or flight mode – releasing stress hormones *and* strengthening fearful neural pathways. Habitual or indulgent fear begats more fear. Our bodies' systems – digestive, nervous, endocrine, muscular-skeletal, reproductive, circulatory, respiratory, and excretory – are designed to work optimally at a 95% parasympathetic nervous system dominance (Simon Borg-Olivier).

The Real Me

This is our rest and digest state; in flow, relaxed and calm. Only 5% of the time we might need our sympathetic nervous response to kick in; to dodge a car or catch a falling item.

For most of us hypervigilant, information-saturated, wide-eyed, sleep-deprived folk, the numbers are in reverse. We're in fight or flight mode most of the time. And we know it. The constant bathing of our cells in cortisol, the anxiety hormone, is corrosive to our organs, reduces sleep quality, lowers immunity, compromises digestive quality, decreases fertility and more.

> *"Curiosity will conquer fear, even more than bravery will'*
> *James Stephens*

There are many practices to balance our fear, stress, and anxiety - our breath and meditation practices, particularly. The goal of this part of the course is to explore your relationship with fear. Fearful behaviour has its roots in evolutionary survival, and we observe some value in looking out for traffic when we cross the road! However, do we cower in the shadows of the complex societal cornerstone fear has become? Everything from FOMO (fear of missing out) to the terror induced by advertisers hawking items we *"must not be seen without"*?

Consider this: The receptors on our cells which bind to the hormone adrenaline and produce sensations of fear, are also the receptors which accept the hormones for excitement. Interesting. At times, could we be mistaking excitement for fear?

> *"We're all afraid of the wrong things."*
> *(Clifton Mark)*

Entering the Dagobah Cave

Let's explore our relationship to fear. You can sit with each of these questions now; some you can invoke in moments when you notice yourself being particularly fearful:

Q: What is my greatest fear?
Q: What are my three greatest fears?
Q: When was the last time I felt fearful?
Q: Do I *not* identify with the word fear but more so with her synonyms/cousins - anxiety, nerves, hesitancy, adrenalin, panic, startled or scared?
Q: Do I fear death? God? Ageing? Loss? Hurt? Challenge? Other people? Falling over? A job interview? Being exposed in some way? The unknown?
Q: In this moment, what fear, if any, am I experiencing?
Q: Am a fearful about my ability to live as *The Real Me*? If maybe, explore.
Q: Am I scared of being wrong? Being seen to be wrong?
Q: Is it possible that I'm interpreting excitement as fear in some situations?
Q: Am I frightened to ask for help? Why?
Q: Do I fear *"what might happen next?"* and not being in control?
Q: Have I had an experience in which fear sharpened my focus and deepened my understanding?
Q: Am I scared of other people's perceptions? Not liking me? Thinking I'm stupid, no good or that I'm too...anything?
Q: Does fear lead to overthinking, over analysing and doubt? Then paralysis and inability to act or decide? In which situation(s)?
Q: Is it possible that fear is keeping me stuck in some way?
Q: Do I justify my fear as protecting myself from a particular outcome? What might that be?
Q: Is there a learned pattern of fear around a certain issue/s? From childhood or observing other's reactions?

The Real Me

Q: Am I scared of experiencing a particular emotion, because it may be overwhelming?
Q: Can I experience healthy balanced fear on a clifftop or an amusement ride?
Q: Do I actively seek thrilling experiences such as diving with sharks and bungee jumping?
Q: Have I experienced strong physical/emotional symptoms such as panic attacks?
Q: How do I respond to fearful situations/aftermath?
Q: How afraid am I to show up as *The Real Me*?

As I was writing this, I spied a baby cockroach crawl around the edge of the dining table, just a few centimetres away from me. In a moment of startle and reaction, I crushed it with my hand. It was a primordial fear. Panic, germs, and infestation of my home. Creepy crawlies. *Yuck*!

Yet a moment later, I was looking at the remains of this little, tiny being and my breath began to gasp and feel completely wrong. My throat felt dry and choked up. This little creature just popped up to say hi, getting on with its own stuff and instead of noticing & mindfully sweeping it gently into my hand and putting it outside, I smashed it.

And I noticed almost immediately that acting out of fear and mindlessness does not feel right in my emotions. It doesn't feel right in my breath. It doesn't feel right in my body. And then came in the emotions of sadness, guilt and regret. And for me, the engagement of breath and letting go.

Pay attention when something similar happens in your day. The little critter was not the issue; I knew this moment helped release and unburden some old and stuck sadness, guilt and regret that had nothing to do with the creature's demise.

Entering the Dagobah Cave

Notice the next time you experience anxiety and or fear. Explore the bodily sensations, hold the space and allow your breath to settle. Explore both the cause and effect. Ask yourself, what can I learn about *The Real Me* and letting go?

> *"Fearful people are more dependent, more easily manipulated and controlled."*
> *(George Gerbner)*

By others, of course. But also by loud elements of MeRightNow which aren't the real you.

If you've strongly identified with fear as a barrier to recovering *The Real Me*, continue to use the Letting go Practice as well as the meditation and breathing protocols daily. Become very aware when the fear response emerges within *You*. Notice the triggers, your physical responses and allow yourself a few breaths, particularly long exhales; take a few moments to enquire further into your experience.

The Real Me refuses to live in debilitating fear yet recognises healthy fear and the continuum of fear in my life. In every moment *The Real Me* is letting go to make space for curiosity, courage, play, gratitude, and openness.

When the only thing left to fear is fear itself, (Roosevelt) recall Winston Churchill, *"Fear is a reaction. Courage is a decision."*

Do we doubt it?

The Real Me

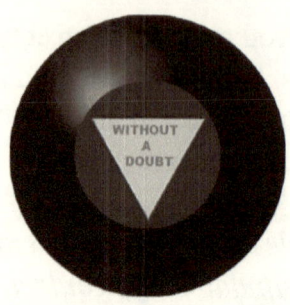

*"Never doubt what comes from the heart, your feelings
know you better than anything else."
(Leon Brown)*

Fear can be a natural evolutionary reaction; we notice, we deal and come back to balance. Doubt, however, can be a sneaky undermining of *The Real Me*. Doubt can keep us buried and not living our full authentic lives. Mis-information and dis-information campaigns don't need to convince us, they simply sow seeds of doubt. Fear generally causes us to act whereas doubt stays our hand. We don't act, don't notice. We dismiss our inner voice, scoff at our intuition. Is there a gaslighter in your life who undermines you and encourages you to doubt yourself, your decisions, your Real Me? Doubt undermines our courage, our resolve and our unique wisdom. It's the Uriah Heep of emotions.

Doubt is to be uncertain about; consider questionable or unlikely; hesitate to believe. For me, doubt feels cold and can stop me in my tracks. As with any inhabitants of our Caves, doubt has its own continuum. I'm still exploring doubt and wondering if intuition and *The Real Me* can sometimes introduce doubt when we intellectually 'think' a decision or action is right but somehow doesn't feel right. Is there a positive face of doubt? Allow yourself to consider.

Entering the Dagobah Cave

General doubt may be a useful red flag and help you tune in to your intuition when a situation, decision or person suddenly feels wrong. Questioning your decisions, motives and understanding is part of a healthy connection with *The Real Me*. Doubt, to the point of general inability to act in your own best interests, is not *The Real Me* and is learned behaviour. Unpack this.

Investigate yourself, learn from your experiences and 'mistakes' but do not doubt yourself.

Self doubt is a crippling incarnation. She will stop you from following your dreams.

Today and this week, tune in to both fear and doubt as you may experience them. Explore and feel them. Notice how they might bring you to act or not. Come back to our first exercise: Do I Trust myself? Sit with this for a few moments. Is your answer similar, different or more refined than your response in the Introduction.

Place yourself generally on the continuum of:

Reasonable helpful doubt _____ debilitating doubt.
Reasonable helpful fear _____ debilitating constant fear.

If you have recognised doubt and or self-doubt as a too-regular and crippling companion, work through these inquiry questions:

Q: Do I trust myself? Keep coming back to this one and explore.
Q: How do I respond to fearful situations/aftermath?
Q: In which situations do I commonly doubt myself?
Q: How do I feel when doubting? In my body? Breath response?
Q: When I feel doubt in my mind and body, can I describe the result? (Long breath then action? Panic? Walk or run away and

not act? Other..........) Is this helpful, or do I have other techniques to release doubt and continue with my day?

Q: Does my doubt have a history? Who taught me to doubt myself? Sit with this one and let go.

Q: Can doubt tug at me after a decision and encourage me to change course or take a different approach?

Q: Can I distinguish doubt from fear?

Q: Do I doubt, then beat myself up over doubting and inaction?

Q: Do I generally experience the doubt, then do it anyway?

Q: Does doubt often, sometimes or rarely leave me frozen and paralysed, unable to decide or act?

Q: Does my doubt become tangled with fear?

Q: Do I experience healthy and reasonable doubt?

Doubt diminishes as The Real Me emerges.

We doubt when we don't know ourselves particularly well and thus we hesitate, rely on thinking and weighing up options intellectually. Our most vital and important decisions are made by our hearts and *The Real Me*.

> *"Our doubts are traitors, and make us lose the good we oft might win, by fearing to attempt."*
> *(William Shakespeare)*

Language — The Cave of Echoes

Helloo! Helloo? In this part of the cave we listen to our own voice. Our own words echo back at us. And we pay attention.

Today is the Day of Words.

Entering the Dagobah Cave

Oh, the power of our words. They can fill us and others with light, acceptance, trust and hope or can be used as weapons of undermining, gaslighting, cruelty and despair. They can soothe, heal and encourage yet burn, cut and decimate. We're exploring both the light and dark side of words: as tools for recovering The Real Me through our own lexicon, as well as how we receive and protect ourselves from language of others.

Words are of course, learned and arise from a continuum of habitual language at one end (small talk?) to mindful *Real Me* conversation at the other end. Words can be central to our communication with others, though tone of speech, body language and our often-subconscious assessment of the energy of others, each play a large part. Words are part of our creative expression of *The Real Me*; playful, compassionate and open-hearted & can channel our Superpowers and more. Except when they don't.

Words are a pale imitation of anything they attempt describe.

Imagine describing the taste of butter to a person who had never experienced it. Our vocabulary places limits on our understanding of complex phenomena. As a student of Adelaide University Psychology in the 80s, I was taught that the Inuit Tribe have forty different words for snow – apparently, there are even more, as there is more than one Inuit language – and these are compounding languages. My point is that each of those words have meaning to the Inuit people. My vocab has four terms for snow: snowflake, powder snow, snow, and ice. My culture, livelihood and personal safety does not require a wider *snow* vocabulary, and I don't use these terms daily. The lesson taught that day stayed with me. The broader our vocabulary, the more deeply we can understand complex ideas.

The Real Me

Ultimately, language is all about meaning, communication and shared understandings. Your communication reflects your experiences, your understanding of those experiences and your personal exploration as *The Real Me*.

All communication is ambiguous, with the listener determining meaning, not the speaker.

This is pertinent in *The Real Me* course as you are both questioner and responder! And both the meaning and responses you will get from these questions are guaranteed to be different to what I have in my head and heart whilst writing.

Every single word I utter has consequences.

Consider the deep truth of this statement both as yourself and upon colleagues, friends and family.

Topics of conversation: what do you talk *about*?

I've come across various articulations describing the following continuum:

The highest form of conversation is about ideas, middle ground talk is about events and the lowest form of conversing is about people.

Of course, there are times we need to talk about people and events; life happens, but consider how often we have open forums about ideas with our family, especially. We trap our girls (aged 14 & 16) around the dinner table and chat about ideas. Sometimes it's illuminating, sometimes contentious, but always interesting. Honestly, if it weren't for those dinner conversations, they'd hardly talk to us and we wouldn't know them at all.

Entering the Dagobah Cave

"Words can inspire. And words can destroy.
Choose yours well."
(Robin Sharma)

Ask yourself these questions:

Q: What sorts of ideas, events (and people) do I talk about?
Q: How would I approximate my ratio of talk between ideas: events: people? Narrow it down to ratios with particular family members, particular friends. Acquaintances and colleagues?
Q: What is my attitude towards small talk?
Q: Do I enjoy challenging conversations - politics, religion and the like, or do I shy away?
Q: Can I respectfully hold space for ideas different to my own with my language?
Q: Can I protect myself from barbs or hurtful language of others?

From ideas to words
Today, our practise will be to use less words than usual and really notice the words we use and choose. And of course, we'll notice the words that others around us choose.

Habitual Language

"Every word you speak supports your perceived reality. Don't put words to the subjects you do not want to add momentum to."
(Abraham-Hicks)

Even as the meanings of your conversations are determined by your listeners, (not by you, the speaker), **below** are some words and word groups I recommend you Recognise in your speech, writing and conversations. These echoes are Shadow Language. *The Real Me* uses and chooses words carefully, respectfully and with an ever-growing understanding of yourself and your audience. After Recognising, you might consider retiring some of these from your vocabulary or simply using them with more care and awareness. If you Allow them, use with caution and consider that they might be less *The Real Me,* and more cannonballs (or soggy tissue balls!) aimed at yourself, or others. As always, the light and shadow are up to you.

- **General coarse language** which may be misunderstood. Use sparingly with awareness.
- **Negative or undermining habitual talk** about others and/or yourself. Common ones: *"Oh that was silly!"*, *"I'm a screw-up"*, *"f@#wit"*, *"what a moron"*, *"don't be such a cow"*, or just plain old *"typical!"* - the list goes on. Add some of your personal labels and un-favourites. Sometimes a terse delivery can turn a pleasant word into an ugly assault.
- **Should/ought**: This is a big one. Notice if and when you use it. "I should" or "you should." When I say it, I notice my face, body language and energy change, and I feel tension in my jaw, between my neck and shoulders and my belly clenching. Experiment on yourself. Experience is knowing. Then trial *"I will"* or *"I may"* or *"you could"* or *"I'll consider that"* or *"that might be a way Forward,"* and ask yourself the questions that arise beneath the shadowy umbrella of *should*. Said to yourself, should may illicit emotional drain - shame, blame, guilt, regret, none of these are *The Real Me*. Said to others, it implies similar emotional load but with you as their judge or advisor.
- **Try**: as *Yoda* says, *"Do, there is no try."* There are many useful words that come from the *"tri"* stem; triumph, trio, and trial are all great ones – by all means test out a particular

technique or food or breathing practise but if you are *trying* to do something, you *are* doing it! Any effort *is* doing, and our expectations of our own/someone else's performance needs to be examined. When I find *"try"* popping out of my mouth, I lengthen it to try-yal. Trial! Let's *trial* it. It sets an intention and has a stronger, more open energy.

- **Expect/assume:** Oh yes. Oh no! Who's expecting what from whom? And most of us have heard the acronym, *assume*; makes an *"ass"* out of *"u"* and *"me."* From where/whom does this sense of expectation derive? Expectation comes from mental and cultural habits, often derived from our own backstory, but not The Real Me. *"I expect so"* is an innocuous phrase and *"expect respect"* and *"high expectations"* can be useful as a parent and teacher, but generally we can model respect, demand respect and have discussions around what respect looks like, without expectation. High expectations? Have them of yourself.

"Assuming is the root of all disappointments."
(Rogienel Reyes)
And who needs it?

- **Can't:** How about upgrading to *"Won't"* or *"I choose not to"* or *"I'm not there yet; still working on it?"* Women who, in many cultures, are rewarded from birth for being pleasant and not upsetting the status quo – have difficulty saying *"no"*, without some kind of excusing phrase. Consider practicing a variety of ways of saying no to someone who will put-upon you/nag you/strip your power (Julia Cameron calls them *"crazymakers"*). Imagine, practise and sense saying no to them — you know who they are — that person who expects the Earth from you, gaslights you and sets a curriculum, teaching you to doubt and disrespect yourself. You *will* find

The Real Me

yourself saying "Hey I can't...." — notice and pay attention when, with whom. Then find other ways of presenting *The Real Me* in these situations. Leave excuses at the door.

- **Perfection**: There is no such thing. You can approximate great or really awesome as perfect, but if you use this as a self-critique, notice from where such self-negation really arises. Aim for success not perfection. Perfect is a mental construct and will distance you from *The Real Me*.
- **Problem:** I like to use the word *"issue"* but play around with this one. A problem is simply an interpretation of an event. Are there other ways to perceive this? At family counselling, we were once told *"If, as a family, you spend a lot of time discussing problems, you become a problem family."* The word became anathema to me, after that. Generally, if you label something as a problem, it becomes one. How about re-assigning it as an issue? Challenge? Opportunity? Which of these resonates with you? Do you tend to say this about yourself *("I have a problem")* or others (*"What's your problem? Any problems here I can help with?"*)? How often do we smile and say, *"No problem!"*? In such cases, this phrase may reflect *The Real Me*; as always, notice how it feels in your body and without judgement.
- **Have to:** Do you *have to*? Habit? Choice? This may be common phrasing for you – notice if you are choosing to do things that feel wrong. Or are you marching to the beat of another's drum? *"I have to be up at 4am for work."* Sure, use the phrase, but regularly interrogate it whenever you notice yourself using it.
- **I'm not:** How about we communicate *The Real Me* – what you *are*. I find this one particularly difficult in our modern world. *"I'm not hungry"* or *"you're not doing* XYZ?" can appear innocent, but straight away you will start thinking about food or *should* I be doing XYZ? Notice when you use

it about yourself, particularly, and notice if and how it ties in with *expectations*. Not can be used as a qualifier, as in *"how do I know what I am, if I don't know what I'm not?"* A *continuum?* Notice.

- **Need/wish/want:** Are any of these your favourites? Notice when they crop up. These words engender a sense of lack. *The Real Me* has no lack; you are learning and adapting, The Real Me is complete in any given moment.
- **Just:** It's a qualifier and may be used to soften a sentence. Sure, it can mean honourable (as in justice, a just person can see both sides clearly and make a good decision), but in general language it's a diminisher. Notice how you use it about yourself? I'm a habitual, serial *"juster"* and am on the lookout for it erupting from me at any given moment. Just? It's gone!
- **But:** Could you use *and*? Say to yourself *"I really want to exercise every day but... (I don't have time, I hurt my ankle – or fill in another ending).* Say it to yourself right now, aloud if you can. How does is feel in your body? If you are like me, I tend to exaggerate the *"but"* into *"buuuuuut"* and my whole energy takes a dive. *"I'm going to exercise each day; figuring out what to do and where to start. Tomorrow I'll..."* And notice how many needs, wants, try's and cant's could so easily get injected into this sentence and you find yourself not exercising. Whatever it is, if it's important (*The Real Me* communicating with you) and you want to trial it — not try it — plan, stick to it, and notice how the experience makes you feel before, during and after.
- **I Don't:** What do you *do* rather than *not* do? Keep your conversations in the positive and notice the difference. Includes *"I don't know"* which can be a lightbulb moment shone on ignorance, whereas alternatively it can be a refusal to engage on a lot of levels.

- **It's not fair:** Includes *"It's so not fair; you're not fair, how is that fair? Life is unfair!"* Where did you pick this one up? From your children? Peers?

> *"Life is not fair. Get used to it."*
> *(Bill Gates)*

Life may not be fair, but *we* can choose to be fair. *The Real Me* chooses fair. We can observe what happens to us, observe our perceptions and learned/unconscious reactions & language around these events, then we can choose to respond differently.

We all make errors and misjudgments. And blurt words mindlessly at times. We notice, and we refine. The words we've discussed and others of your personal lexicon will come dancing out of your mouth quite gaily today or tomorrow — and possibly for the first time you are really going to notice. Pick one or two which really resonated with you to begin dismantling. And, as always, begin now.

The present moment is the only thing that's actually Real.

Being the observer of your own and others' language can be a game changer.

Zero Tolerance For Abusive Language

If others attempt to control us by landing verbal blows, we are going to feel the hit. If these verbal barrages, put-downs or gaslightings stem from unconscious patterning of your boss, colleague, friend, or family member, it will still really hurt. Notice where you feel it in your body, this gives you a moment to process, but not accept it. It can be tempting to re-form some of the armour we've been

Entering the Dagobah Cave

releasing, especially if a friend has stabbed, blindsided or physically winded you with their words. Or if the speaker is attempting to shame you in front of others. Take a breath and let it go slowly. Smile and let it go again. Refuse to accept the ballistic energy the other person is leveling at you.

Consider that the haranguing has its source in their own hurt or habit. You may feel compassion and feel brave enough to say, *"Stop. I don't accept that."* You don't need to give a reason. Barraging back will not make you feel good and will deplete your energy further. Conversely, Accepting this material without a word will teach others how to treat you and lodge in your body as, *"I deserve this. I'm not good enough."*

Do not *accept. Stand your ground, feel strength in your body from a calm breath and respectfully reject the assault.* Then walk away. This sort of response may have its own consequences but does not result in you giving away your power and depleting your well-being. Notice how you feel later; five minutes later, half an hour later, later into the evening. Do you find yourself ruminating, replaying, *"I should have said* XYZ" and mentally nursing, but reliving the past in the present? Keep practicing Letting go and know *The Real Me* was there, in that moment.

And allow silence.

Allowing the Silence

This part of the course is not about silencing *The Real Me*; it's bringing attention to and noticing habitual elements of your speech and conversation which were never *You* in the first place. Do you feel comfortable or uncomfortable in silence and begin to chatter about random things? Unlearn and re-learn, and we'll do it concurrently, whilst noticing frustrations or discomfort arising at any moment.

Approach this part of the practice with the same detachment and non-judgement that we've been practicing throughout the course so far. Let go of any emotion of disappointment or beating-up of yourself when habitual language pops out. Notice, smile, relax your body, and notice your next breath:

Inquiry questions: What are my language habits, and do they reflect *The Real ME*?
Q: Do I not attempt noticing language because it's just too hard and pointless?
Q: Where do I place myself on the continuum of
Good _____ Poor communicator?
Q: When I notice an "I should" or "don't" (or *your* 'favourites') arising from myself or others, am I able to notice, smile, relax and breathe?
Q: In which situations, times of day, or emotional states do I find myself using more mindful language?
Q: In which moments or circumstances do I find myself using more habitual language?
Q: Have I rephrased sentences when noticing shadow language?
Q: Am I paying more attention when others use shadow language?
Q: Can I play with language; be curious and creative? Notice when language is in flow.
Q: Do I feel the need to fill silences with any old chatter?
Q: Have I experienced flow in my language and communication?

Have an interesting week sitting in each of these cave spaces. Enjoy the challenges and the exploring.

Entering the Dagobah Cave

Continue your breath and meditation practise each day & creativity and play.

Have you identified other caves spaces you'd like to explore? Feel free to write your own questions, or contact me for revisions in 2nd edition.

> *"Self-enquiry involves turning toward and learning from the very experiences we want to avoid, discount, or find challenging."*
> *(Jason Luoma)*

Chapter 9

Being The Real Me, Each and Every Day

"Why should I be untrue to myself?"
(George Harrison)

Having journeyed this far into the book and engaging with the exercises in the course, you will have noticed yourself being *The Real Me* many times in different situations, recognising feelings of openness and lightness, fullness and wonder, space for *The Real Me*. You may have noticed yourself being more observant, engaging more with family and others from a fresh perspective. Creativity and playfulness will be prodding you and you'll be responding.

You'll also notice times, issues and situations where you habitually or automatically drop into *Not Me* and you've felt this discord in your body and breath. Heaviness and contraction. And being able to *let it go.*

Q: Choose one situation in the last day or two where you noticed yourself *not* being authentic. How did you respond and re-route your engagement?

No judgement if you didn't Let go or re-route. Awareness is the first, singular and great light.

You're also noticing your habits more keenly. Some habits might even have started crumbling or transforming simply through the power of your attention. You will also have noticed times and events when fatigue, clutter, fear, a habitual response, doubt, or ignorance saw you crash and burn for a few moments, an hour, a day or maybe a few days; you've taken the time to Recognise, Explore, Accept and Let go, whilst using the tools of the breath, meditation, and awareness. I for one, am very excited with the progress you've made so far. Allow yourself to be pleased, too.

Being The Real Me. *Is there any other Me to be?*

In this chapter, being *The Real Me* Each and Every Day, we'll extend; moment to moment, day to day, week to week, and year to year. You are the accepting and accountable archaeologist/renovator/inquisitor of *The Real Me*, probing and inquiring, sometimes decimating the boundaries of the *Stuck Me*. In Chapter 9 we will expound some nourishing routines that you can use to scaffold and support your recovery of *The Real Me.*

Depending on your personality, routine can sound like a super-boring loaded word (me) or a bastion of necessary structure without which I'll fall apart (my husband). You'll be somewhere on this continuum. Together, we'll explore daily, weekly, monthly, and yearly guides to refining practices which are nourishing, grounding and balanced, and supportive of *The Real Me*.

Most important are the daily routines, or I as like to call them daily *practices*; whatever we prioritize; day in, day out. *These are the foundation of your being The Real Me in the world.* These practises must be grounding, nourishing and balanced; every day (almost) without fail. We don't want to do so much as to exhaust ourselves or do so little as to enter into lethargy.

As *The Real Me* unfolds we can explore and commit to our balance; from daily foundations, we can begin to scaffold weekly, monthly, and yearly practices which will find you living each day, more authentically as *The Real Me*.

Continuously Conscious Choices

Daily, weekly, monthly, and yearly scaffolding of our lives.

Let's get out of 'Busy' and 'Habit' and get into living conscious authentic lives.

We're returning to the ideas and awareness of Chapter 1, maybe eight weeks ago or more & noticing what we're doing each moment and asking ourselves "Why?" We'll explore our routines and look at implementing simple systems to get the most Me in our everyday. You might like to review Chapter 1 or jump straight in.

For me personally, I find the daily routines the most challenging because I tend to be the sort of person who likes variety and naturally lean towards haphazard. I generally loathe Timing and timetables because I want to do everything now. I used to get up in the morning with a head full of a zillion things that I wanted to achieve that day. And of course, one never achieves a zillion things in a day, and by the end of the day, I would often feel despondent at *how little* (Oh, look, judgement!) *I'd achieved*. Now I simplify my list of things, continually remind myself to enjoy them *whilst* I'm doing them (flow) and make continuously conscious choices about what tasks and people I will engage with. And I use the *One, Two, Four Method*, which we'll explore soon.

And some days I'm more The Real Me in flow than others. Acceptance.

It's been a long time since I've said, *"I was so busy today, I didn't get to shower."* I make sure my self-care time is paramount, as this is the deepest part of my daily foundation. This includes my morning meditation, breathing and walk/run/Yoga (I like variety and it depends on how I am feeling).

We're going to make a list of your daily, weekly, monthly, (biannual) and annual important self-care activities. I'm also going to introduce you to a method devised by my friend Wendy Trevarthen, called the *One, Two, Four Method*.

These strategies will assist you to connect and engage deeply with your day-to-day activities, and within each task, remain deeply rooted in each moment and as *The Real Me*. Commitment to *The Real Me* will take exploration and practice, and remember you can't do it wrong. But you can forget or neglect to do it. Times in which you need more self-care, you'll notice and respond — no apologies necessary. On energetic or super-scheduled days, you may find yourself overextending; notice and adjust.

The first 20-30 minutes in the morning. Grounding.

Being The Real Me, Each and Every Day

Let's look at some theory and practice, and we'll start with some of my personal morning routines:

Tongue scraping upon rising and a big glass of water/lemon water with medication (Oroxin - GP prescribed medication for Hashimotos Syndrome, Thryroid condition). For one hour in the morning, I do a varied combination of breathing practice, meditation, walking, running and or Yoga practice. Depending on the day, I'll do more meditation, less running or more Yoga, more running, less meditation. But I commit to giving myself that one hour. Yes, sometimes I'll do a whole hour of breathing & meditation in bed because *The Real Me* has those days.

What are your general morning routines?

First-thing in the morning, self-care is super nourishing and grounding. However, if your grounding time is in evening, go with it. Caring for myself physically, mentally, and spiritually grounds me in *The Real Me*. During and after self-care, I really feel like *Me*; I've taken care of myself and then I can move into the rest of the day. Personally, since I've committed to morning self-care practice, others benefit as I'm less rushed, cranky and distracted! I'll then shower, make a cuppa, get the girls up and make breakfast.

Your daily morning Self-Care routine must be simple and doable. If you wake up anxious, as I did for years and start your morning stumbling around with a coffee in hand, ask the question:

Q: What do I *need* to feel grounded in *The Real Me* when I wake?

Listen, and keep asking the question if you're feeling blocked. You can self-inquire every morning, like I do and find yourself sitting for breathwork or meditation, or lacing your running shoes. If you're still not sure, trial 10-20 minutes of *any positive, grounding activity* that has felt good for you in the past. Then allow yourself to flow into the busyness of your day.

The first 20 minutes or so after waking is when your brain waves are still in the relaxed alpha state, (8-12 Hz) which you might recall is also brain wave frequency of flow.

Your morning self-care is a time investment that engages The Real Me and benefits everyone with whom you will come into contact during the whole of today.

You might already be exploring your five-to-ten-minute breath and meditation practise each morning. If not, have a go. If you reach for your phone immediately upon waking, consider postponing for twenty minutes or so and asking yourself: *What Self-Care practise do I need this morning?*

Dailies. The Real Me Blueprint.

What routines/priorities keep you Real every day?

Your daily routines are your blueprint for your life.

Here are mine.

Sarah's Daily: My morning grounding as discussed above, eating fresh food, drinking water (six cups), one cup of coffee, three (or more) cups of tea (I love my chai!). Warm hugs, stroking pets and smiles every day - both giving and receiving. I make my bed. I look for at least one opportunity in a day to assist somebody else. Sometimes anonymously. I create and eat at least one nourishing meal with vegetables; eat at least one piece of fruit. I eat away

Being The Real Me, Each and Every Day

from my workspace (mostly!) I look for an opportunity to share; occasionally on social media, though more usually with family or colleagues. I connect with at least one friend or family member not living with us. I read something that interests me. Chat/play with my children. Tell family members I love them. Laugh at something amusing. Play/move outdoors. Create *or* clear something. Read something. Rest twenty minutes (afternoon is when I'm less productive, so a twenty-minute rest at 2 or 3pm is heaven). Be in bed by 10pm. Finish the day with zero emails in my inbox... still working on that one!

So that's my daily list. Anything I do above that is a bonus, and that includes things like my work. The work I do at school, the work I do for the business and my writing. I do set myself five to six work hours per day and work hard to stick to six hours. It helps me prioritise and not work late into the evening as I used to do as a high school teacher.

Who are the really important people in your life who regularly deplete your self-care Real Me balance and work/creativity priorities? No prizes for guessing family & friends, community, pets and or kids, and/or partner. These are super important and teach us the skills of contributing to the lives of others assessing their needs and balancing with our own.

My boys are independent, bless them, and my girls are teenagers so they don't need me as much anymore. But I really want to stay connected with them and support them when they *do* need me or want to chat. One of my priorities is to drop what I'm doing when they come in the back door or out of their bedroom. Give them my full attention whenever they actually come to me for a chat. Eat with them whenever possible, and tune in. And the same with my husband. Yes, there never seems to be enough hours in the

The Real Me

day, and every day brings its own joys and challenges, with plenty of give and take. Your life too will have crazy days where the day you planned is 180-degrees from the day you're living (Lockdown 6pm today! Get food! Send emails! Make sure everyone knows!) You know how it can be.

*Get your Dailies en pointe and you **are** The Real Me*

To regularly forgo your dailies (or not to have them) is to invite burnout and fatigue. Not to have solid self-care routines and work boundaries is to age quickly and invite chronic illness. The Real Me is begging you to turn the love and care you lavish on others inwards to yourself.

Exercise: Gently allow yourself to notice and record your Dailies.

Q: What are my non-negotiable dailies?

Dig deep and start with a list of three or four. As you move through today or tomorrow, add to your blueprint as you notice the important parts of your day which scaffold everything else. Keep moving through your day, keep adding to your list. Pay attention to tasks, pauses, notice when you get up and need a walk (did you really need the cuppa or did you simply need to get up and move? Talk to a colleague at the water cooler? Stare out of the window for a few moments? Release a big sigh or exhale?) *Notice what you do,* as you might not generally notice or think is important. Maybe it's not, maybe it is; keep paying attention. This will be a working list. Then each day, this week, play around with your blueprint. Extend, shorten, love and create.

Solidify your dailies by the end of this week and this becomes *The Real Me Blueprint*. It is who you are.

Refine and continually create The Real Me Blueprint, create your life as you want to live it. This is Real Me Resonance. Revise in six months or a year as events, work, family, and life changes. Notice what does NOT change.

At one very low point in my life, my only daily goal was to not get angry. Anything else was a bonus. Seriously. A very heartfelt and special thanks to all the people who were compassionate to me during the times I was the furthest away from *The Real Me*. Begin where you are.

"We must use time as a tool, not as a couch."
(JFK)

Weeklies: The Real Me Scaffolding

What routines/priorities keep you grounded and moving forward in The Real Me, every week?

Let's swan-dive straight into the weeklies: things that you do every week, or that you feel *The Real Me* is nudging you to do regularly, though not necessarily daily. These are the foundation and walls growing up from the daily priorities of your blueprint.

Sarah's weeklies: A weekly Yoga class where I participate as a student in a class; ninety minutes, and personal learning; two hours. Whether it's a podcast or a blog that I'm reading, or some articles, a book or a documentary. Often, it's more than two hours, but always a minimum of two hours of personal learning time. Home Yoga with my husband at least once a week.

A walk-up Mount Gravatt with my husband - this moved into dailies when I was working from home! Catch up with a friend or family member in person, sometimes phone or Zoom.

The Real Me

Creative time: Two hours, again; that's a minimum in a week where I block out two hours. I'm either writing or I'm drawing, painting or gardening, reorganizing something or designing a room. Something creative; two hours. Post on social media and email my Centenary Yoga community with updates.

Chores: Laundry used to be once a day with four children at home; now a bi-weekly plus lovely hubby does most of the laundry. Clear out one drawer, shelf, or part of the house (dark corners) because I'm still in the middle of clearing out stuff. Vacuum (love the Robot vacuum). Organise dinner, though I might not be preparing or cooking each day. The general house clean.

Shopping at the markets: I love to be surrounded by all the fresh food and the chatter and the energy and the people and food and the smells and the coffee. It's something I love to do with my husband on a Sunday morning. I always cook a special meal for the family once a week. So, it might be a roast or salmon, might be something vegetarian. But I try to get everyone together once a week and sometimes it works, and sometimes it doesn't.

Playing, always an hour or so, sometimes games with family/children or handstands or playing guitar, or dress-up. Sometimes Solitaire with my favourite Nepal deck of cards.

Work: I have certain face to face work hours when I'm school teaching, teaching Yoga in the studio and two hours of business admin and planning each day.

Family: At least one family dinner at the table, as most nights at least one of us has an evening activity; at least one family activity to reconnect. With teens preferring to avoid us, it's mandatory!

Your weeklies might include a sleep in or breakfast out on a Sunday morning and, your weekly shop, baking, a sweep or some gardening or a trip out in your dinghy. Let's write:

Exercise: Gently allow yourself to notice and record your weeklies.

Q: What are my non-negotiable/desired weeklies?

List 3 or 4, or dozens of weeklies and add to your list as you traverse this week. Feel into the important parts of every week; the walls (or clear crystal structures) which support your showing up as *The Real Me*.

Each Month: The Real Me Rooms:

Bringing to light the beautiful hidden spaces

Monthly Self-Care practises are those least likely to see the light of day. Read that again.

Monthlies can be super-nourishing & important parts of The Real Me. Sarah's monthlies are things I'm drawn to do every month. This is important scaffolding, but really easy to skip or keep re-scheduling. The dailies and weeklies or randoms will muscle in. For me, monthlies are events to look forward to, and really help to nourish me so that I can then interact more fully as *The Real Me*. Like? A Massage each month. Finish a book I'm reading within a month. A Restorative or Yin Yoga session each month. Often, I facilitate a Deep Restorative Yoga session once a month. A monthly might be a visit to the movies, a gallery or hairdresser/barber. It might be a day on the beach or a hike with family or friends. It might be a gathering of family/friends for a BBQ, birthday or a date night with your partner. It might be a Zoom meeting with colleagues or a monthly report for work.

Monthlies can be work, creative, family and Well-being. Of all the monthly strategies we notice and implement, which ones do we somehow *not* get around to doing this month? The Self-Care routines, I'll bet. So be on the lookout for those monthlies you really enjoy, those that nourish you and in which you realise you haven't engaged or participated for months!

Optional scaffold:

Quarterlies/biannual: The Real Me Gardens

I've added these in as they may be important scaffolding for your Real Me.

Every quarter of the year, I try to visit some family who's either interstate or not local. Also include things like visits to the dentist and car services. BAS statement. A weekend retreat. A camping trip. A movie or trip to the opera or festival. A local theme park or visit to Zoo. An extended timeline for a creative project. Clothes shopping for the season.

Quarterlies can lend themselves to family, cultural and fun events; thus 'the Gardens'.

If you have children, quarterlies will naturally pop-up during school holidays. If you have fur-kids or are empty nesters, do you have any quarterly routines or special nourishing activities?

Q: Do I have quarterly activities? How do they contribute to The Real Me?

Yearlies: The Real Me Lighthouse or Chandelier

Being The Real Me, Each and Every Day

What overarching activities guide your year?

Yearlies set our tone and direction. Our beacon might be an overseas or interstate holiday, holidays in general, Christmas or cultural letters, parties and events, blood tests, health check-ups, and insurances check-ups. Tax returns. Pet vaccinations. New work clothes or Yoga/gym gear? New work or relocation. New intention or resolution.

Q: What are my important yearly activities? How do they contribute to the Real Me?

As before, write down three or four that immediately spring to mind and or heart. And as today progresses, set an intention to recognise your yearly landmarks which are important to you. And if we pivot on a yearly vacation, how else might we *Real Me* this void?

If you choose, you can explore each Yearly to find out more about *The Real Me*. Let's use a holiday as an example:

Q: Do I take a yearly holiday as a habit?
Q: Do I take a yearly holiday as a break from routine?
Q: Do I take a yearly holiday as I love planning and envisaging myself or family in these spaces activities?
Q: Do I take a yearly holiday to explore and learn?
Q: Do I take a yearly holiday to sleep, eat and relax?
Q: Do I not take a yearly holiday and for what reasons?
And additionally;
Q: Which yearlies might I let go? Which don't serve me anymore?
Q: Which yearlies might I like to adopt and explore to find the boundaries of The Real Me?

This week, take some time to sketch out your dailies, weeklies, and monthlies. Perhaps quarterlies and yearlies. Allow these to be small, manageable tasks, little chunks of *The Real Me-time* perhaps. Simply write down two or three of each **right now;** often getting started is the biggest challenge (or is that just me?)

During the week, explore what you do each day, (re-use the awareness exercises from Chapter 1. What am I doing? Why am I doing this?) with even more attention and intent; no judgement. Notice *feelings* and flow around your daily activities. This will be a big clue as to whether you're showing up as *The Real Me*. If it feels right, you're in flow; engaged, relaxed, and *The Real Me*.

> *"Don't tell me what your priorities are. Look at how you spend your time and you'll know what they are."*
> *(Adapted From Henry W Frick)*

Returning to the Dailies - The One Two Four (1,2,4) Method

Work with this section of Chapter 9 if you'd like to explore scaffolding your Dailies a bit more. Let's talk about the *One Two Four Method*. This technique is borrowed from my friend, author Wendy Trevarthen. This is a *Daily* method to assist you in exploring your priorities. Again, whatever we achieve, it's coming from a place of being nourished and balanced.

First, Wendy says to *"place a number 1 next to the most challenging thing you want to accomplish in the day."*

The number 1 is tagged next to an achievement, scaffolded over and above your foundation practices.

> *"List one outcome that is non-negotiable."*
> *(Tim Denning)*

Being The Real Me, Each and Every Day

For me, it might be writing a chapter, or it might be getting through a pile of marking or weeding a section of garden. Or a family picnic, booking a weekender or making a special dish from a recipe that's a bit different. This must be *the* most important thing or challenge that you want to accomplish in the day. Something that you know is going to take you probably a couple of hours or more, so the greatest amount of energy and most of your time and focus for that day. If you're painting, it might be painting a room. Or if you're clearing out a room or clearing out a wardrobe, that would definitely be number one. This is the 1 in the *One, Two, Four Method*.

For me, and many of you, number one is work. Four to twelve hours depending on your day. But what about your non-workdays? Number One can simply be to relax, grocery shop, mow lawns or visit a friend. And if you are retired, what is your one? It could be your painting project or creative work or ... (fill in the blank).

"Place a number 2 next to two other things that you want to achieve in the day, but you know are going to take less time and a bit of effort. So, things that could take from ten minutes to half an hour."

Or maybe a little longer. Two things that you really want to accomplish in your day. For me, it might be scrubbing out the shower because I tend not to clean the bathroom when I do the rest of the house. Or cooking a meal. Or chatting to my Stepdad or a friend on the phone. Or updating spreadsheets or helping one of my girls with a bedroom clean or playing a game. An afternoon walk. Two things.

"The list of 4 things as you might have gathered, comprises of small things that you can accomplish that day."

The Real Me

- **1 = one task - non-negotiable - two hours or more**
- **2 = two tasks, half an hour each**
- **4 = four tasks, fifteen minutes each**

These might take you five to fifteen minutes to do. They're things that if you don't get done today, it doesn't really matter that much. You can add them to the 4 list for tomorrow. Have at least one of the 4 that you intend to achieve. Renewing your insurance, paying a bill, booking a massage, washing dishes, sending an email or text. The 4s can be urgent, important or both. They can also be neither, yet something on your to-do list.

Beware of the time balloon out, especially if, like me, you are a self-confessed awful estimator of how long things take. It's common for one of my 4's to expand into a 2, especially if I find myself in flow. Play with the 1, 2, 4 Method and see if it resonates with you. No hard and fast; simply exploring.

The 1, 2, 4 Method is a way of prioritizing your very valuable time during the course of a day. Of those things, your number one, on one particular day might be your two hours of creative time. That might be what you prioritize; that's what you're pouring all your energy, your creativity, and your spirituality into for that day.

So, whether your number one priority for a day is your creativity or not, keep or allocate some time for your creative Me; You showing up through your art, whether it be music, writing, drawing, cooking, creating, and the list flows on. It's about simply showing up as *the Real Me* through your art, time and flow.

This week as you jot down your ideas for your routines; ask yourself the questions:

Being The Real Me, Each and Every Day

Q: *What do I need to support myself being Me?*
Q: *What do I need to do to support myself being Me?*

What do I *need* and what do I need *to do* in my day to day living and being *Me?*

Make it a mantra; and note what answers come up, in your mind, body, numbers and any other way The Real Me *communicates with you.*

Keep adding to your Blueprint, your paths, your Rooms, your Gardens and your Lighthouse as you flow through this week. You may be surprised at the size your list by the end of the week! Then start culling. Keep thinking about the things you want to work through, the weeks and the months as the Real You emerges each new morning, blinking into your own light.

Inquiry Q: What's my relationship to The Real Me, each and every day?

Q: Am I able to regularly start the day with simple, grounding nourishing routines? With no judgement if I don't?
Q: Do I generally end a day feeling satisfied and accomplished?
Q: Do I generally end a day feeling I've lived it as **The Real Me**?
Q: When yes, what emotions arise, if any? How does it feel in my body?
Q: Do these days typically involve flow?
Q: Did this day (today) typically begin with a realistic plan? 1,2,4 plan or other?
Q: Did I notice *not* being in flow when things went wrong or not to plan? Or am I in my best flow in these moments?
Q: When I'm not able to work to my priorities, what emotions arise? How do I feel in my body?

The Real Me

Q: When gazumped, am I able to Breathe, Recognise, Accept, Explore and Let go? Ask for help? And then move on?
Q: Am I able to share my triumphs and troubles and feel listened to? Do I listen to *myself* in a nourishing way?
Q: Am I able to fully relax at the end of a busy day?
Q: In the evening, do I reflect on the interesting elements of my day; non-judgmentally, then let them go before sleep? Journaling is a great way to 'close the book, close the day' before sleep.
Q: Am I able to present an authentic calm, energized and relaxed *Real Me* when with others?
Q: How does it feel to be *The Real Me*?

The Real Me has interests and talents and valuable work to do. Doing a variety of tasks, creative and play, caring (for Self and others) and managing our environment are all parts of *The Real Me*. Feeling good about oneself in *any* situation is a hallmark of *The Real Me*. Ultimately, what I see *out there* reflects what is *in here*; a beautiful, compassionate, creative, caring *Me*.

> *"So happy I don't have a fake image to maintain.*
> *Some days I'm amazing, other days I'm a wreck but*
> *everyday I'm me."*
> *(Connie Harris)*

Chapter 10

Running Away With The Real Me or Me, Next...

> *"Oh, the places you'll go!"*
> *"Congratulations. Today is your day. You're off to great places. You're off and away. You have brains in your head. You have feet in your shoes. You can steer yourself any direction you choose."*
> *(Dr. Seuss.)*

You're noticing *The Real Me* showing up in most areas of your life. Productivity, creativity, and balance. You're feeling more grounded and more nourished, implementing routines, and choosing your attention with care. You're noticing different words coming out of your mouth; perhaps less words, perhaps more meaningful conversations.

The Real Me

You're transforming before your own eyes and the perceptions of others. You might be dressing a little differently or a lot, smiling more often at nothing. Saying 'thank you.' Being more playful and relaxed in your approach to tasks and to others. Spending more time in different activities and flow, as you explore creativity and living with more space. And Peace. Allowing some things to fall away. Discovering, accepting and being *The Real Me*.

Running away with *The Real Me* is continuing to explore the concept of *The Real Me* as a path into your desired future: destiny, perhaps? It's **not** a goal that's somewhere out in the future. It's not a time or place or Graduation Day for which you are to strive! It's not a test and it's not easy. But it can be very, *very* simple to Breathe, Recognise, Explore, Accept, and Let things go. And tune in.

As we highlighted at the very beginning of the course, *The Real Me* is always *MeRightNow*. So, where you are right now **is** *The Real Me*. And yes, a few chapters ago, perhaps it was a lot more concreted, diluted, stuck and scattered, but right now you're living as *Me*!

With every new experience and choice, whilst living an engaged and attentive life, The Real Me evolves.

The *Me* you imagine yourself to be in twelve months or five years will still be *The Real Me* but not exactly as you are today. Imagine yourself even more authentic, creative, compassionate; peaceful and joyful as your *Real Me* emerges more fully. And you're more likely to evolve into this future *Me*, (*Me, next*) if you have some sense of what *Me, next* might be.

> *"I know for sure what we dwell on is what we become."*
> *(Oprah Winfrey)*

Running Away With The Real Me or Me, Next...

Ponder that for a moment. Let's return to the idea that *The Real Me* is MeRightNow. The magic of *MeRightNow* is that in this moment you are simultaneously being *Me* plus laying a path toward your *Real Me* future. What do you want this to look like? Feel like?

Let's work this chapter with an intention; a statement about where you'd like elements in your life to lead. Where *would* you actually like to go? Oh, the places you'll go! Let's dream a little.

Imagine your ideal life or you living your dream life. What would your Real Me be doing right now? This afternoon? Tonight? Tomorrow? Next week? Next Year? In 5 years? Where are you? With whom?

This may be the most difficult part of the course, as it's really hard to imagine a life we've never experienced. Movies, magazines, books and podcasts may help but we don't 'know' it because we haven't experienced it in our bodies and our lives. For those who are parents, can you remember planning for your first child? Or planning a holiday or planning a career when we were in high school. All the research we did! Our experiences of new things are rarely what we *expect*, and expectations pave the way to sameness and habitual thought patterns. We simply can't know what a new experience will feel like moment to moment until we're *living in* those moments. The mind will barge in with 'but I thought...!' Keep your awareness sharp and open. Feel into these moments and experience flow. Leave the judgement to others. Trust that you'll know.

We're going to reach deep into *The Real Me* with imagination and intuition to explore the Ideal Me. Okay, that may sound scary and weird. The Real Me... now the Ideal Me? This is precisely the reason why 'Running away with the Real Me' is almost our last chapter together. We're taking everything we've learned via inquiry and experience into

The Real Me

paving our own Yellow Brick Road, paver by paver, brick by brick in the directions that *The Real Me* really wants and *needs* to go. We're discovering, allowing and accepting our Real Me imperative.

Bye-bye comfortable rut, let's pave our way into my Real Me future.

We are going to explore systematically. Cautiously or gung-ho, we will begin by partitioning your life and lived experience into eight different sections. I'll name them for you. Then you'll be invited to dream and intuit your ideal life *as it may feel if you were actually in it/ doing it/ living it* for each sector of your life. Your Real Me is the strongest and most authentic it's ever been right now, so tune in to *The Real Me* to explore & create your current ideals. Take it slow and easy with curiosity, compassion, and courage, the Real Me Superpowers you've been practising.

In each section, you'll be asked the same question:

"In my ideal or dream life, I am..."

The purpose of this extended exercise is to really tune in to how it *feels* to be in your ideal home, work, relationship - and the rest. In a moment, I'll introduce you to the 8 facets or categories of Me we'll explore.

To clarify what this exercise is *not*: It's not a way for you to tap into what you *think* you *should* be writing; thinking is grey and always comes from the past and it's easier than imagining our future. This is tough, honest, authentic work and is the pinnacle of *The Real Me* process. Don't be hesitant to dream BIG!

Avoid overthinking. There are no correct or incorrect answers, ideas or statements. Write down whatever flows out of *The Real Me*.

Running Away With The Real Me or Me, Next...

You don't have to show anyone else, but you must show yourself.

Generally, what comes up from your deepest places in *The Real Me* is right for you in the current phase of your life. We're exploring and it's soul.

In each sector, you can give one response or more; short or long responses, as feels right for you. We'll call them *intentions*. An intention is like a resolution; an idea we create in the present which opens up a pathway into tomorrow and the next day and so on.

If you can, dot-point your intentions as this will be helpful for part B.

And yes, you can do this, even if you're not confident, skeptical or a bit scared. Even if you come back to it later (schedule it as one of your 2s (from the 1,2,4 Method) tomorrow!) Even (and particularly) if you think you don't know what you want, or if you're not sure if you can even articulate or imagine it. You've come this far! Take 5 relaxed breaths, tune in and Trust yourself. Allow yourself a few minutes now or later to do these exercises. You have an enormous level of agency as to who your *Real Me* is tomorrow, next year and in 10 years' time.

If someone else's life depended on it, I know you would do it. So do this for yourself.

Remember, there are 8 sections of your life to explore, and if my partitioning doesn't resonate with you, ask yourself the questions and set your own landscape for this work.

Let's do number one together:

The Real Me

1. **Personal relationship or partner.** *"In my ideal or dream life, "I am..."*

Read it again. Note that this is not 'In my ideal or dream life, *my partner* is....' Consider how You are in your ideal relationship. Close your eyes, *Feel it,* **what does it feel like?** What does it look and sound like? How are you showing up? If you're not currently in a committed & stable relationship, what might that feel like?

And yes, there may be some non-negotiable qualities & values that your partner/relationship simply must have. But this is about you.

Allow some ruminating and let answers bubble up from deep inside where answers come. Write down your responses and let *The Real Me* do the talking.

Now let's work the same process with the other seven categories in your life.

For each, don't overthink. Allow yourself and write down 1, 2 or 3 (more or less) feelings, visions, words or sentences that come up for you. If you draw a blank or a difficult emotion comes up in any category, hold the space and move on when you are ready. A 'blank' or an emotional watershed can be most informative when we're ready to explore and ask questions around why, then really listen.

Take around two to five minutes for your first draft of your Ideal List to limit overthinking and allow it to be free writing. Here we go!

A. The 'Ideal' List

1. Personal relationship or partner.   *"In my ideal or dream life, "I am..."*
   ➤
   ➤
   ➤

2. Family.   *"In my ideal or dream life, "I am..."*
   ➤
   ➤
   ➤

3. Home, the place I live.   *"In my ideal or dream life, "I am..."*
   ➤
   ➤
   ➤

4. Work.   *"In my ideal or dream life, "I am..."*
   ➤
   ➤
   ➤

5. Friends.   *"In my ideal or dream life, "I am..."*
   ➤
   ➤
   ➤

6. Leisure.   *"In my ideal or dream life, "I am..."*
   ➤
   ➤
   ➤

The Real Me

7. Creative   *"In my ideal or dream life, "I am…"*
-
-
-

8. Spiritual.   *"In my ideal or dream life, "I am…"*
-
-
-

How did you go? Spiritual we've covered last, not because it's least important but it can be difficult to define thus can draw a blank with some people. Spirituality can be broad, deep and unique to you. How you nourish yourself spiritually can be anything from your connection to land and country, to a deity (god or gods), your nature walks, Yoga practice, getting to the gym as well as your *Real Me* time. Meditation or prayer and breathing practise. The time you are spending working through this course. Your connections to others. Your gratitude and service. Your creativity and meaningful work. These may all be part of your personal ideal spirituality.

Q: Did you find difficult emotions — sadness, grief, anger, bitterness … coming up in any of these 8 sectors? If so, as always, notice what's emerging and then feel free to explore or put this one aside to return another time. Come back to noticing your breath and smile.

Running away with the Real Me can be fun and illuminating and can also brings up unresolved issues, hurt and damage from the previous Me. We're running away *with* not running away *from*. It simply isn't possible to be *The Real Me* in our ideal and everyday lives without facing, healing and letting go of this old mud and concrete.

Running Away With The Real Me or Me, Next...

And now, some more inquiry questions:

Q: Did you find this task daunting? Exposing? Hard?
Q: Is there overlap between some of your responses?
Q: Any sectors in which you drew a blank?
Q: Do you notice any consistency or strong themes between sections? Explore this.
Q: In which sections did the answers come easily? Why might this be?
Q: In which sections were your responses cloudy? Very broad?
Q: Were any responses specific and crystal clear?
Q: Were any responses a surprise?
Q: Were any responses simply *"to be as things are right now"*?

Take a few moments now, get a drink of water or a cuppa, do one of your "4" activities to clear your mind for a few minutes and then come back and look at your responses. We're not going to do anything more with them for the rest of today. You might even find yourself returning to them later and adding or deleting. And if you cross anything out, use a single line because you can explore later why you chose to omit it. Is it because it was a *should* or an ideal that somebody else would like you to be?

My mother always wanted me to be an air hostess and I was quite clear in saying, *"I don't want to be an air hostess."* So, be very aware if any responses are somebody else's dream for you, or perhaps it *was* your dream once and you've outgrown it, or completely changed your interests or path.

So, we're going to put the list away for a full day; tomorrow you can come back to your Ideals.

Next, whenever you are ready, you are going to *rank* each of your Ideal intentions on a *Short List*, before we finalise your *Real*

List. This will be a "2" activity and will take around half an hour. Let's work:

B. The Short List

Under the 8 categories, you may have 30 intentions, maybe 15, possibly just 8 (if you've written one for each).

From here we create our **short list** by comparing *each of the intentions in each category with each other*. This enables us to Rank our intentions in each category. This might sound confusing so let's start with: Category 1. Relationship.

Say I have the following intentions under Category 1. Relationship: In my ideal relationship, I am .....

1. Attracting a partner who is warm, kind and great with kids (one of mine from a few years ago).

2. Being open and respectful

3. Showing up as The Real Me

4. Having a date night once a week

5. Practising listening and understanding in any conflict before seeking to be understood (from Steven Covey).

Which is Tops? Choosing your Top ideal in each category.

If you have more than one intention in any category, a solid way to rank these is to compare 1. and 2. in your list and to simply consider,

"If I could only have one of these, which one is the most important to me?"

> Attracting a partner who is warm, kind and great with kids?

or

> being open and respectful in my relationship?

Of course, all the points you've written down are important to you and your vision of *Me, Next*, so this is difficult. Make your choice; feel it; record it. Explore it if you will. This ideal is now your **Relationship Number 1.**

Still within the first category, Personal Relationship, now compare your **Relationship Number 1** with 3.

Next compare Your **Relationship Number 1** with 4.

Next compare Your **Relationship Number 1** with 5.

You now have your ***Top Relationship 1.***

Yes, maybe you could have picked it without the structured comparison tool but sometimes we surprise our habitual/thinking mind.

Next, compare all the intentions recorded under *"2. Family"* and ask yourself the same question: *"If I could only have one of these, which one is the most important to me?"* Compare Family 1. and family 2. to identify your **Family Number 1**. Make your choice; feel it; record it. Then compare **Family Number 1**. with all other family ideals you've recorded. This will be your ***Top Family 1.***

The Real Me

Continue down your list for all 8 categories, until you also have ideals, labelled **Top Home 1**, **Top Work 1**, **Top Friends 1**, **Top Leisure 1**, **Top Creative 1 and Top Spiritual 1.**

Perhaps take a break now. You've done well.

Let's list the Top & Short List!

List your **Top** Ideals in each sector below, noting the opportunity to update in 12 months. You can return to the process earlier if you like; 3 months or 6 months.

Top and Short List

	Date	12 months from initial date
Top Relationship 1		
Top Family 1		
Top Home 1		
Top Work 1		
Top Friends 1		
Top Leisure 1		
Top Creative 1		
Top Spiritual 1		

Table i: Top Intentions for each sector 1

Fantabulous work!

Take a break and take a few moments to complete a breathing exercise or short meditation. Return to the next exercise tomorrow, or if you're in flow, lets move into our absolute finals and drive *The Real Me* home.

Comparing your most important Ideal between Categories: Ultimate Finals of The Real Me.

Now we're going to determine *your single most important Ideal/ Intention* from all those you've flagged so far. Begin a third list beneath the second. Now compare **Top Relationship 1** with **Top Family 1**.

Consider, *"If I could only have one of these, which one is the most important to me?" Tough question I know. Take a breath and trust. Your chosen ideal is* **Final 1**.

Compare **Final 1** with **Top Home1**. If you could only have one of these, which would be most important. This is your new **Final 1**. Now compare **Final 1 with Top Work 1**, and so on with the remaining four. Your **Final 1** may be replaced with your **Top Home 1** or **Top Spiritual 1**. If so, this will be your new **Real Me Absolute Final 1 (table ii).**

Your **Real Me Absolute Final 1** is your number one most important, heartfelt, yearned-for Ideal and Intention for Me, next and MeRightNow.

> *'The first secret of getting what you want is knowing what you want'*
> *(Arthur Hlavaty)*

Congratulations for getting to this point. You've made choices comparing each and every couplet. I know some of these choices were no-brainers and others enormously difficult. If you find

The Real Me

yourself being nagged from a deep inside space to revisit any of these pairings, listen carefully before revising:

Q: Is this revision coming from the Real Me? or habit? or someone else's version of me? Consider.

Remember, none of these intentions need be immediately actionable. We spend so much time responding to the wishes and desires of others, *The Real Me* can be deeply buried & ignored, and loosening this compacted energy around Me, who I am and what I want may take some revisits. Use your meditation and breathing practise time to explore any blanks or sticky or stubborn comparisons.

If you're reading this far and have not yet acted on these exercises, consider why not and take 2-5 minutes and write down your Ideals.

Your **Real Me Absolute Final 1** is top of your list, front and centre. Please write it in the number 1 space in The Real Me, table ii (Real Me, Ranked). You might want to post-it note your Absolute Final 1 on your fridge, bathroom mirror. You may wish to share it with a friend or family member.

Now, we'll work the same magic by comparing each of your remaining Final intentions.

1. Choose any of the 7 non-ranked categories; say ***Top Leisure 1***.
2. Compare this intention to all the un-chosen intentions from each of your **Top 1** categories. Whichever comes up as your most important, now compare with the other 6 on your short list. This will be your **Real 2** area of your life on the ***Real Me final*** List.
3. Repeat step 2 for each of your stated intentions.

Running Away With The Real Me or Me, Next...

Congratulations! You now have clarity around which of your 8 short-listed intentions is your heart's greatest desire and a general ranking. No judgement if you 'think' Family or your spouse 'should' be at number 1 or 2, or even top 5. *You are simply exploring your strongest desires which need to be expressed in this moment.* Your **Real Me Absolute Final 1** may simply be something crucially important which has been buried the longest or deepest.

You now have your **Real Me Absolute Final 1** and your other **Reals** order. Complete your Real Me Final List below:

Real Me, Ranked

Number/ Real	The Real Me _____ (your Name) Final Intentions for each life category. DATE:_____ IN ORDER AND BY ORDER OF THE REAL ME.
RealMe Absolute Final 1	
Real 2	
Real 3	
Real 4	
Real 5	
Real 6	
Real 7	
Real 8	

Table ii: Real Intentions, ranked

The Real Me

You now have a list of eight or more facets of your ideal life in rank order sitting in front of you. Ask yourself:

Inquiry Questions:

Q: Are my ideals modest in some categories and huge in others?
Q: Do these intentions look right? Feel right?
Q: Am I inspired by this process? Exhausted? TERRIFIED?
Q: Is there anything missing that I may have blind-spotted?

The Ultimate Real List

At this point, you think you're done and might be dismayed to see another table on the next page. As with anything in this course, it's purely optional. Yes, I know I said you *have* to work the Real list but you and I both know, this work can only come from the Real You. And you've done it.

There is a final step and some of you may have already intuited what it might be.

Let's say I have three full-on, super-important, creative, tugging-at-my-entire-being intentions under my Work (or Creative) category that *I know* need to be 1, 2, 3 on my list before I even start comparing Family 1, Spiritual 1 and the others. Are you following? When I first explored this exercise ten years ago, I had nothing from *Relationships* or *Work* in my top ten! That told me a lot. Interestingly, looking back, my **Real Me Absolute Final 1** was to create a Wellness space in the Western Suburbs to serve thousands of people. Back then, my work was high-school teaching and now I work in my Yoga business. So now I can categorize this intention as my Absolute Real 1 under Work. At the time I saw Work as my job as a high school teacher!

Yes, you can work your Ultimate List intuitively but if you find the systematic approach helps you bypass your thinking mind and get to the heart/soul/*Real Me*, here's how you do it:

1. Revisit each Intention from your **Real Me Top 1** *category.* Let's say your ***Top1 category*** is Work, to follow the example above and maybe you had four dot points. You've identified your **Ultimate Real 1** from this facet of your life.
2. *Now look at your next dot point under this category.*
3. Compare this dot-pointed intention to **Real 2, from Table ii**. Whichever comes up as your most important, now compare with Reals 3- 6 on your short list. This will be your Number 2 on the **Ultimate *Real Me final* List**.
4. Repeat steps for each of your stated intentions under the same **Ultimate Real Me Final 1** *category.*
5. Write your **Ultimate Real Me Final 2** in Table iii.
6. ***You're on a roll!***
7. Now repeat steps 1-5 for your **Ultimate Real Me Final 2** *category,* comparing each un-chosen dot-point from Real 2 with Real 3, Real 4 down to Real 8
8. And continue with **Ultimate Real Me Final 3** *category* dot points and so on.

You now have your pathway forward into the Real Me, as The Real Me, by The Real Me.

The Real Me

Number/Ultimate Real	The Real Me _____ (your Name) Ultimate Real Me Final Intentions. In order and by Order of The Real Me, Date:_____
Ultimate Real Me Final 1	
Ultimate Real Me Final 2	
Ultimate Real Me Final 3	
Ultimate Real Me Final 4	
Ultimate Real Me Final 5	
Ultimate Real Me Final 6	
Ultimate Real Me Final 7	
Ultimate Real Me Final 8	

You've done it! Take a moment of quiet celebration.

In this moment, you have shed illusions of your NotMe and stepped into the light of your *Real Me*.

Running Away With The Real Me or Me, Next...

Now, it's up to you to continue - or begin, living these intentions, front and centre. Today, when faced with any choice, and it's usually about how we spend our time, choose in favour of your Ultimate Real Me. Can you challenge yourself to begin living as *The Real Me,* today, right now?

Your life is the ultimate demonstration of your priorities.

Inquiry Questions:

Q: Do I have more than one intention from any of the 8 categories? What might this suggest?
Q: Do I have an even spread? If no, what might this suggest?
Q: Are some categories noticeably absent?
Q: Do these intentions look right? Feel right? Reflect *The Real Me*?
Q: Am I inspired by this process? Exhausted? TERRIFIED?
Q: Is there anything else that may be missing that I may have blind spotted?

The Real Me snapshot
Your *Ultimate Real Me Finals* are a snapshot in time. Right here, right now in fact. Will they change? Of course! As your life changes, you realise your goals and your interests diverge or narrow. As your understanding of yourself broadens and deepens, you will discover and uncover buried and surprising aspects of *The Real Me*. What could be more fun, meaningful and joyful?

So work through the Real Me process again and again, maybe as one of your chandelier, 1,2,4 tasks in 12 months. I'm ready to do mine again now and see what my *Real Me* has to share with me moving forward.

The Real Me

Choosing The Real Me
You've mapped out and blueprinted your priorities above. Now, each and every moment, each and every day with direct access to a myriad of choices and opportunities, choose your path from your heart; from the list above; choose to be The Real Me.

You may have some very big dreams. And perhaps you have no idea how you could even get there. Release the *how* for the moment and focus on the *who* and the *what*. Clarity about *who* you uniquely are and *what* you can uniquely contribute and care about, will walk you into your future with clear blueprints to guide your choices.

The *how,* your path forward, is created through your choices, micro and macro choices. Choosing in favour of your ideals, choosing to show up as The Real Me. Choosing to support your dreams as well as your physical, emotional & material well-being; each day, each moment.

"It's not our abilities which show us who we truly are, it's our choices."
(Albus Dumbledore (J.K. Rowling))

Whatever might come up for you, if it's strong and authentic, and benefits both you and others, then it's already part of *The Real Me*. It's as simple as that. And *The Real Me* has ways of removing the roadblocks and throwing opportunities into our path, nuggets which will map out our Ultimate dream list as destiny's path into our ideal future. And help us to discover Ideals and parts of The Real Me we didn't know existed and are waiting for us to find them.

Every minute, every day, make those choices that align you to your Ultimate Real Me.

Running Away With The Real Me or Me, Next...

For some of us, it's a big sea-change, tree-change, career change or relationship change. The scales falling from our eyes. And some of us act swiftly. Our *Real Me* has been in the waiting room far too long! Others may take some time musing and in planning of small or larger changes. Let's face it, if you leave a corporate job to teach paddleboarding or pursue your Art, move to the seaside or leave/cement a relationship, there may be some real logistical issues with which to contend. You may downsize, move, re-jig finances and your day to day timetable may change. Surprised family members and friends may not be as supportive as you trust. Whether we make sweeping changes or simple but different micro choices each day to release *Ultimate The Real Me*, your life will evolve into a more *Me* shaped life. How we approach our awakening to our path forward will be as individual as each of us.

Choose in favour of *The Real Me* and your Ultimate list as above. Print a copy and place it where you'll see it numerous times every day. Bathroom mirror? It can be private, or you can publish it (or parts of it) or share with your greatest supporters for more accountability, and a cheer squad.

It is our CHOICES, in each moment, to align ourselves with our deepest desires, creative passions and authentic purpose; these choices strengthen us and connect us with The Real Me.

Remember, you can't do it wrong, but you can forget to do it. You can find yourself in ruts and habitual fog, fugue and fatigue. *Or* you can be living your best life as *The Real Me*, paying attention, learning, being curious, creative & feeling gratitude; sharing your gifts and loving your life.

Oh, the places we'll go! Enjoy every moment, the opportunities, the setbacks, and the triumphs. Notice the triumphs! Revel in the flow and the journey. Of course, *The Real Me* doesn't identify with any of it; *The Real Me* simply delights in being alive to experience it all.

Identifying the elements that are most vital to The Real Me is paving the yellow brick road with a solid path in the right direction.

This might seem like the end, but I'd like to complete your mission with explorations of relationships. What do other people have to do with *The Real Me*?
Everything.
Don't believe for a moment that you can do this alone.

Further Reading:

Some ideas in this chapter were drawn and refined from Janet Bray Attwood and Chris Attwood "The Passion Test" (2004)

Chapter 11

The Real Me, Meet The Real You

"You can't fully become yourself by yourself."
(Claire Zammit)

Relationships are the basis and the foundation of our existence in this life. Relationships are connection. Relationships are complex. Relationships give us some of the most awkward concrete slabs that we must shift to climb out of the old, encased version of ourselves. Relationships assist us to lean into living our most authentic life.

Our final *TRM* chapter is about connecting with *The Real Me* through our relationships, using our relationships as a tool, as a mirror, and asking questions about those many relationships. We're going to shine a light on what our most challenging relationships (as well as the pleasant ones) tell us about the exposing of ourselves as we really are, or about the way we tend to run, hide or armour up. Do our relationships show courage or fear, gratitude or expectation? Are we open or closed?

So, let's start with relationships with other people. (If that seems like an odd sentence, bear with me.) If you're having issues or what you perceive as problems with a romantic, family, or collegial relationship — and who doesn't — a lot of that will revolve around *"he said, she said," "he did, she did"* and *"can you believe that they did or said that??"* And generally, you get a whole chorus of your people who are shocked and horrified and completely agree with you, stating how they can see, *"this must be a difficult relationship for you."*

Then you may dig deeper and notice lots of blogs and quotes explaining how the best way to improve your relationship with anyone else is to begin with yourself. That can be confusing when, obviously, the other person and *their* behaviour, values, and demeanour are the problem. Again, stay with me, because we ARE going to start with *Me*.

> *"The most important ingredient we put into any relationship is not what we say or what we do, but what we are."*
> (Steven Covey)

The Real Me philosophy, quite simply, is that everybody you meet is *You*. Yes, really.

In this chapter, I want you to consider everybody you see, meet or connect with as *Me*, but a me who has experienced a different set of parents/ guardians, culture, different upbringing, and wholly different life experiences. If you'd been born in their family and lived their upbringing and had their experiences, then they might have been *You*. Everyone you observe and interact with, everybody at work, everybody you see at the beach, the park, out playing, or in a lift... *Everybody* is perhaps simply a different version of yourself.

He is *Me*. *She* is *Me*. They are Me.

This open and accepting mindset is a way of releasing judgment of others, moving away from fear of others, challenging yourself to look at the values of others, accepting others, and closing the gap of that pervasive illusion of separation. It's a philosophy that returns us to being and feeling connected; with our partners, our friends, people at work, and particularly people with whom we've had a what-we-would-call-difficult-relationship.

"Often the only sacrifice we must make to feel a greater sense of connectedness is convenience."
(Jeff Krasno)

So, if relationships *are* the cornerstones of our existence, we want to strengthen those foundations. At the same time, realize that those foundations of relationships with others are a mirror of our relationship with our *Self*.

As you've worked through the course, you've done the work of inquiring within yourself, noticing, experimenting, and exploring yourself. Consider the idea that the curious love you've extended to yourself during the course, can be extended to others; the idea of inquiry, the idea of exploring, the idea of listening and practising without judgement. The idea of speaking your truth, the ideas of courage, gratitude, and playfulness. Are we able to extend to others these courtesies, these necessities, every time we show up as The Real Me *with somebody else*?

Let's break these practises into steps:

Step one: Explore the idea that everyone is *You*. Every person you met is a conversation you're having with yourself had you lived a different life, so why not explore their ideas?

Step two: Withhold judgment. The mind will be very, very 'in the ego,' and be very, very keen to jump in and make judgments about how that person is not like us. They're different to us. Why do we believe that? Rather, are we able to accept the person for who they are and accept them with an attitude of love?

Step three: Bring an attitude of love and acceptance into every interaction.

Your last assignment for our last chapter together is to pay attention to the way you behave in your relationships, your interactions with anyone and everyone this week. Let's begin with some general relationship questions. Work through these with an intention of inquiry and flow:

Q: Am I able to compassionately consider relationships in my own family? Those role models who have *taught* me relationships?
Q: What are my beliefs around relationships and are they true for *The Real Me*?
Q: Do I consider myself *good* at relationships? Why? Or why not? On what might this depend?
Q: How do I display care in my relationships?
Q: Do I allow others to care for me? In what ways?
Q: Do I protect myself in my relationships? How?

The Real Me, Meet The Real You

Q: Am I able to show respect to those with whom I disagree?
Q: When might I decide to terminate a relationship? Can I speak my truth compassionately to this person?
Q: What factors make my best relationships strong?
Q: How do I feel about difficult relationships I may have experienced?
Q: Is there one relationship that I will work with today that needs some level of healing? (It doesn't mean you have to necessarily do any healing, but consider how *you're* showing up.)
Q: How would I like to see myself showing up, coming face-to face with a person with whom I have an unhealed or difficult relationship?
Q: Picture a relationship which is particularly triggering. Explore. Then perhaps choose another.

"Someone else's opinion of me is none of my business"
(adapted from Rachel Hollis)

You can't change anything about someone else's perceptions of you, but you can consider how you show up in that environment.

"People will come into your life for a reason or for a season or for life."
(Anon)

Whether you believe that *"some things are meant to be"* or not, consider that people who come into your life, including those you have invited and not, those you have the opportunity to add meaning to, those who have added meaning to your life, or to whom you've chosen to reveal parts of The Real Me. Visualise a person or two who fits into each of these categories. Come back to your breath and sensations of your body.

The Real Me

One of our struggles may be that some people turn up for a reason or a season, whereas we might want them to stay for life. They may not. Others may want this from us and we don't. The deep truth is that each of us are whole and complete in ourselves, but we are unable to realise it because we haven't experienced it. Plus, we're not taught to realise, accept and expand into our own magnificence.

In school, we learn skills to conform & make us useful in society: not to be curious, notice, love and accept ourselves, though some school programmes and teachers work these 'soft skills' into their curricula; conversely, we're not taught to love and accept others (and our environment) *as a part of ourselves.*

So, to find the parts of *The Real Me* which remain hidden to me — my blind spots — I put myself in relationships with others. Parents teach me about myself, yet only in the ways they've learned, and we inherit and are taught their blind spots, plus a whole lot of baggage! (Based on Marianne Williamson's teachings.)

It's a paradox that we are each intrinsically whole and are unable to recognise it. Yet we're getting there. Paradoxically, we're all parts of a whole and each of us can help to heal each other, whole.

The Real Me Process helps.

Someone will turn up in my life that I'll be able to mentor because there will be some part of their life in darkness or some part of them that is buried or fractured (un-whole or unhealed) in an area I have worked on or have generally discovered more of *The Real Me*; thus, I can help them simply by being *The Real Me*. Other people will turn up in your life who will help to lead you or to heal you in areas where there is darkness, ignorance and confusion. Many of these relationships are not the warm, fuzzy kind; they are vital, nonetheless.

The Real Me, Meet The Real You

The aim of relationships in our lives is to help each of us to transform into ourselves.

The Tough but Important Relationships

Consider whether my core relationship beliefs present ideal relationships as being like Shangri-la, rainbows and lollipops, drifting around with harps, whilst smiling at each other. Happy Ever After fairytales. Is that my idea of good relationships? Are we completing each other's sentences, enjoying the same things, never disagreeing? Or are we present in those relationships when someone inconveniently needs us, when they've disappointed us, when they are pushing our boundaries? Are we in these relationships with kindness, allowing others to also ask us the tough questions; allowing them to see our bits of *The Real Me* which are still under excavation and that we might not feel ready to share?

"Relationships are like saying wordlessly to another person, 'My rough edges, meet your rough edges.'"
(Marianne Williamson)

Relationships are that space between me and another person, which isn't *Me* and isn't them. It's a space between *Me* and you into which either of us can add deposits and nourish and/or make withdrawals. Some of your tougher relationships may be consistently in the red, and there may be those into which I feel I deposit continually – and they simply withdraw.

The challenging, but important relationships are those we may spend most time ruminating about and going round and round in our habitual behaviours. And they tend to be within families; we would likely not maintain friendships with such challenges in the mix. And intellectually speaking, we know that we're responsible for our own behaviour, not that of others, but can we really understand and experience this awareness in a heated moment, when we feel disrespected and powerless?

Practising *The Real Me* in my Relationships

If we stay with the idea that the other person really is Me & that relationships are all about assisting the reclaiming of *The Real Me*, we might notice that our relationships give us endless opportunities to practice being *The Real Me* – daily. I'm continuously receiving feedback from both my own relentless self-observation, as well as from other's responses as to whether I'm showing up as *The Real Me* in every conversation, gesture, text and decision which involves others.

Sometimes I'm horrified at how badly I fail. Non-judgement, non-judgment! And the incredible compassion of others to Accept me is humbling. I Recognise, Explore, Accept, Let go. And then I move into the next moment, the sine-wave of our emotions bringing me back to balance, having experienced *the Real Me* in both the highs and the lows. The glare of our compassion and shared humanity. Who we really are!

When in doubt, kindness is the greatest of all virtues.

Relationships provide so much material for *The Real Me* to feast upon; for this reason, I like to call relationships, *"Manure For The Real Me Mushroom"*. Or if you prefer, they can be, *"Sunlight for The Real Me Sunflower!"* We can begin to perceive every relationship interaction from a shifted perspective. Reciprocally, we can assist others into their *Real Selves* simply by being our *Real Self*. We become the light in other people's lives to help them develop; to help them explore and emerge, simply by exploring our most authentic *Self* around them.

When relationships, or moments in those relationships show up and push our buttons and trigger us in some way, that's great! What better opportunity to notice physical responses? Tension, breathing change, wide eyes, heart racing, yelling, crying, throwing things, sulking, silent treatment, door slamming; fight or flight coping mechanisms. And it may be another person doing these things– and/or it may be me! There may well be habitual patterns in a relationship where simply by noticing and altering my response, a blind-spot or galaxy sized-hole in the fabric of this difficult relationship may begin to change and repair. In the midst of awful behaviour, you may suddenly see someone else's pain and experience compassion. And if so, I also notice *The Real Me* more whole and present in that very moment.

The skills of self-observation you have been practising over and over again will enable you to observe your buttons being pressed in a more detached manner and enquire into your unconscious responses, as well as emotions arising; does this relationship/interaction trigger unholy emotions of unworthiness? Self-righteousness?? Anger? Pride? Loss of control? Sadness? Shame? Guilt? General unsettledness to the point you can't even articulate it?

That's a lot to consider in the course of a single challenging interaction. Noticing one element is a start. One moment of detachment and stepping back is a start. A simple breath is a start. Ask yourself these simple questions:

Q: Am I being self-righteous and walking out because I've lost control?

The Real Me

Q: Am I experiencing shame because this person has brought up *that* event yet again? Are they doing this to control me?
Q: Am I in The Real Me right now? Flow? Or Flunk?
Q: Am I indulging in behavior which generally elicits a response I don't want? If yes, explo*re*.

Return to the REAL protocol in each case. (Take a breath), Recognise, Explore, Accept what's happening right now then Let go and allow the energy in the interaction to shift. With practise you may find that you can smile, work through the REAL process and pivot within that first breath.

Exercise

This may take around five minutes.

Choose a person with whom you occasionally (or often) experience relationship difficulties and imagine (or recall) an interaction with this person, in which you identify that your *The Real Me* had evaporated or left the building. You can warm up by choosing someone who is not integral to your life or choose a person who is both important and will be in a relationship with you for the long haul.

With awareness of *not* getting emotionally entangled, are you able to mentally screen or watch a replay of at least part of your version of that interaction? Notice opportunities for REAL protocol that you may or may not have taken. Allow your body to be relaxed and view the situation again, imagining you choosing *Real* in those moments and noticing your compassion, breath, pause and pivoting. What are you saying now that is different? How is your physical body feeling in this second imaginary interaction?

The Real Me, Meet The Real You

Allow *The Real Me* to end the interaction. What did that look and sound like? How do you feel on completion? Feel free to journal or muse on your Real Me realisation/s from this experience.

Let's move into our final rounds of inquiry questions:

Q: What does this experience teach me about myself now?
Q: Am I able to express kindness and compassion to this person *and myself* in this moment?
Q: How does this expand my experience of *The Real Me*?
Q: How have my response and emotions to this trigger subtly altered since last similar trigger?
Q: How did this experience feel in my body — this time compared with last time, or the very worst time?
Q: Is this a relationship in which myself, or someone else is stubbornly stuck and not healing?

These challenging relationships are going to help us reconnect ourselves with *The Real Me* within our own daily lives; to expose and to excavate the *Real Me,* both for Me and those important people to me.

Esther Perel says, *"The quality of our relationships determines the quality of our lives."* So, let's explore a few more questions (gotcha!) to help us consider the quality of our relationships:

Q: How is this person experiencing *Me*?
Q: How am I experiencing this person?
Q: Do I bring acceptance, warmth, good energy into my interaction with this person? How is this person interacting with me? Is this person interested in interacting with me or talking at me? Deadpanning me?
Q: Am I in a relationship with this person to get something?

The Real Me

Q: Am I bringing *The Real Me* into this relationship with this person?
Q: Can I be honest about who I am?
Q: Do I listen to them?
Q: Do I want to get to know the *Real Them* without judgment?
Q: Do I create a safe space in my relationship with them?
Q: Can I keep myself safe and set boundaries in my relationship with this person?
Q: Am I guarded with this person? Can I explore why? What would happen if I relaxed a bit more with this person?
Q: How would I like to relate to this person? Do I have an act/mask that I put on with this person?
Q: Is this a person with whom I simply cannot have a relationship? Why?
Q: Do I feel I can trust them to care for me?

Allow these questions to surface during this week, particularly with a person with whom you perceive a difficult or distrustful relationship. This is a person who will spark your rough edges or has a way of detonating your trigger points. Notice any tension in your body. Notice your breathing. Notice how you're feeling in your body. Stay in the moment. Ask yourself:

Q: How am I showing up as The Real Me?

Now, consider somebody in your life either currently, or as a past relationship, someone who's particularly special to you. And let's consider that this special person has a strong connection with your heart. Why is this person/relationship special and strong? Are you connected by a multitude of shared experiences? Is it the way they are able to accept you ? Even in difficult situations when you've perhaps done something wrong? Is it the loyalty they have shown to you or courage and caring displayed in a variety of situations? Now consider how can you create space which makes others feel

The Real Me, Meet The Real You

accepted, loved, and unguarded whilst creating boundaries and keeping yourself safe, too.

Narrow down the questions to maybe 3 or 4 which resonate with *The Real Me* and your wholeness. Keep them in your awareness. As you step out of your bedroom door or front door today (or Zoom Call) and come face-to-face with people, keep these questions in mind and consider how you show up in your relationships. How do you manage the relationships or the Me elements of the relationships that you observe? Are you being in the absolute present moment with each person that you choose to interact? Notice those people with whom you choose not to interact. Consider why you've made that choice. No judgment, simply noticing that there's always going to be **a reason**.

Every time you show up as *The Real Me*, you are bringing a sense of love into any situation; a sense of warmth, acceptance, aliveness and real meaning. And there will be moments of courage, curiosity, fun, flow and gratitude, and hey, guess what? You'll notice.

In time and with practice, they'll become part of the fabric and flow of the moment, your day, your year, and your very existence.

> *"Our greatest work is to break free from the inner fragmentation so that we begin to see the unified field that is everywhere, and allow for the unfolding masterpiece to come forward which is our Life."*
> *(Michael B. Beckwith)*

Love your life.

Live it as *The Real Me*.

Epilogue

You are the experimenter, the experiment-ee and experiment.

So, what do you suppose The Real Me actually *is*? Perhaps your soul? Your heart? Your spirit? Your higher self? Some time-warped energy imprint? A tiny piece of the Divine? Let me know your thoughts and ideas!

Here are the Questions with which we began our journey, eleven or more weeks ago. You can compare with your earlier responses or simply feel into how you respond right Now.

Q: Do I love my life? In this moment? In general?
Q: Do I love myself?
Q: Am I willing to explore the idea of *"I'm simply not where I need to be right now and maybe I don't even know where that is"*?
Q: Am I willing to explore giving myself permission to be myself? Am I fearful of what I might expose?
Q: Can I even consider living life as my most authentic self; If no, are there some clues as to why not?

The Real Me

Q: Do I deserve a full, satisfying, and authentic life?
Q: Can I use every day as part of the exploration of building success and staying with it?

And a few more:

Q: How is my life different now?
Q: Do I feel more authentic?
Q: Has this translated into lifestyle changes, contentment or being more present?
Q: Am I better placed to answer the Q Who Am I?

I would love your feedback on the course and feel free to pass your copy on to anyone you feel might benefit from it.

Sarah

Afterword

Today is the day when everything changes.

Right now is the moment.

Coffee and chicory. One single breath and clarity.

Health. Breadth. Depth. This is me.

Not new but reborn.

Not better but more.

And less.

More authentic

Less drawn, pale and straggly.

More round, rosy and together.

The Real Me

More me.

And then more and more me.

Every moment

The Real Me.

I'd love to hear your feedback and experiences during and after the course. Email me at

sarah@centenaryyoga.com.au

Sarah

Notes

The Real Me

Notes

The Real Me

About the Author

Sarah Mills is a contemporary author of both ancient and modern understandings. She loves learning and doing, and has only recently finished high school, after teaching biology, physics and chemistry for thirty years. Sarah is currently immersed in the teaching of Yoga and growing a Yoga community (Centenary Yoga) in the Western Suburbs of Brisbane. She is married to Dr David Mills, who keeps her grounded and is her Rock. Sarah has four amazing children and two stepdaughters, who, together with thousands of pupils, have taught her most of what she knows. She is passionate about Yoga and helping everybody find their *Real Me*. She might write a novel, or two, next.

www.ingramcontent.com/pod-product-compliance
Lightning Source LLC
Chambersburg PA
CBHW030256100526
44590CB00012B/415